HOW-TO COOKBOOK FOR COLLEGE

HOW-TO COOKBOOK for COLLEGE

Easy Recipes *and* **Simple Techniques** *for* **Healthy Eating**

CHRISTINA HITCHCOCK

PHOTOGRAPHY BY ELYSA WEITALA

ROCKRIDGE PRESS

For general information on our other products and services or to obtain technical support, please contact our Customer Care Department within the United States at (866) 744-2665, or outside the United States at (510) 253-0500.

Rockridge Press publishes its books in a variety of electronic and print formats. Some content that appears in print may not be available in electronic books, and vice versa.

Interior and Cover Designer: Brian Lewis
Art Producer: Samantha Ulban
Editor: Annie Choi
Production Editor: Andrew Yackira
Production Manager: Martin Worthington

Photography © 2021 Elysa Weitala

Food Styling by Victoria Woollard

ISBN: Print 978-1-63807-938-5
eBook 978-1-63807-266-9

R0

To my mom, for everything that she has taught.
Thank you for your unending support.

CONTENTS

Introduction ix

CHAPTER 1:
How to Get the Most Out of College Cooking 1

CHAPTER 2:
Cooking 101 17

CHAPTER 3:
Breakfast 35

CHAPTER 4:
Sweet and Savory Snacks 47

CHAPTER 5:
Quick Salads and Sandwiches 65

CHAPTER 6:
Solo Meals 83

CHAPTER 7:
Feast with Friends 101

CHAPTER 8:
Desserts 119

Measurement Conversions 130

Resources 132

Index 133

INTRODUCTION

Welcome to the *How-To Cookbook for College*.

As I was growing up, cooking became an increasingly important part of my life. I have always loved to experiment with new foods and flavors, and now, playing in the kitchen is one of my favorite things to do, whether that means simply trying a new ingredient, making variations on tried-and-true recipes, or creating all-new recipes.

Learning how to cook during my teenage years was an invaluable skill. Not only did it help me become self-sufficient, but it also taught me skills that have carried over into other parts of my life. I learned how to be more organized and prepared and to exercise patience. Plus, cooking taught me that I can explore my creative side with delicious results.

My goal for this book is to help you become more confident in the kitchen while exploring new foods and flavors. Not only will you learn how to make healthy, delicious meals for yourself, but you'll also acquire valuable skills that go beyond the college classroom, such as budgeting, planning, and organization.

Whether you have cooking experience or are brand new to the kitchen, you'll find within these pages a wide variety of delicious, approachable recipes, some of which will remind you of home, and some that will help you spread your wings and try new things. The recipes were carefully designed for the college kitchen: I incorporated various cooking styles with smart uses of pantry staples and base recipes that can be used to make multiple dishes.

I hope this book inspires you to get into the kitchen and create delicious meals for yourself as well as your friends and family.

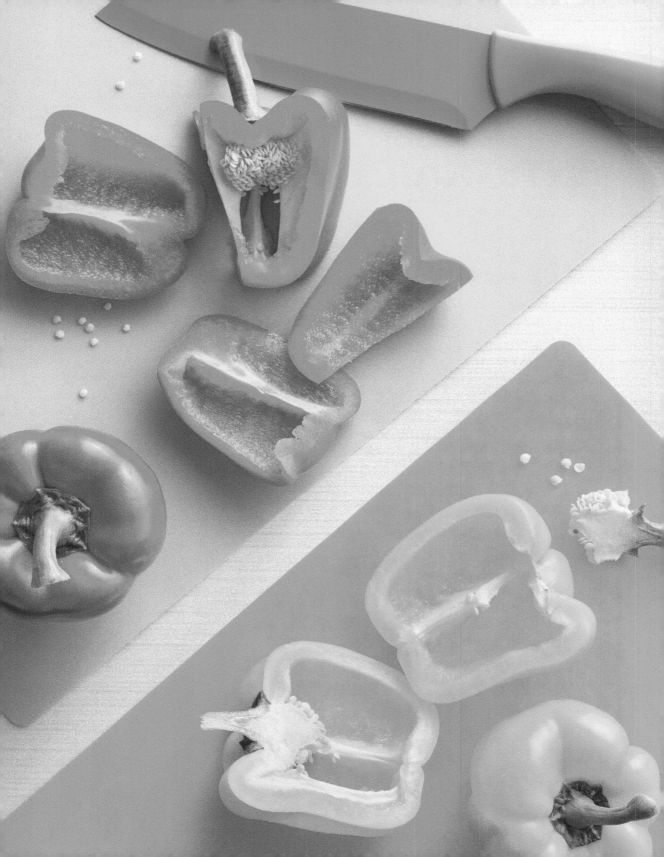

CHAPTER 1

HOW TO GET THE MOST OUT OF COLLEGE COOKING

Whether you have access to a kitchen with full-size appliances or simply a microwave and mini-fridge, you can whip up flavorful and wholesome meals for yourself and your friends. This chapter will show you the best ingredients to stock up on and the equipment needed to get started.

Why Cook in College, Anyway?

Your college years are a time to experience new things and learn about yourself. Much of what you take away from your time in college will be lessons learned outside the classroom, and the knowledge you gain will carry you through the rest of your life.

College is a great time to learn how to cook. Whether you have access to full-size kitchen appliances or only a microwave and refrigerator, you can begin learning basic cooking skills. Cooking for yourself is an affordable alternative to expensive takeout and boring dining hall menus. It's healthier than subsisting on prepackaged foods, because you can control what goes into your food and how it's prepared. Cooking is fun, too! It allows you to experiment in the kitchen and can be a relaxing way to take your mind off stressful coursework.

Cooking in a college setting can be different from cooking at home, however. With limited access to equipment, space, and groceries, cooking in a college setting takes a little creativity. But with the right recipes and techniques, you can satisfy your cravings any time of the day—or night. You won't be reliant on dining hall hours or limited menus. And, if you run out of meal plan credits, you will be able to fend for yourself.

Cooking your own food provides an opportunity to explore new flavors, try different foods, and master new skills. And, like most other skills, the more you practice, the better you become. I encourage you to try the recipes in this book. Then, as you get more comfortable, you can play around with the flavors and ingredients and make the recipes your own, which is the best part about cooking.

Cooking is something many people learn to love in college. Not only does cooking for yourself give you a sense of independence, but it also brings people together. Cooking and eating with friends can be a great bonding experience. Whether you're cooking for your friends or with them, the best part is enjoying the fruits of your labor together.

Whether you're craving something meatless, healthy, sweet, or a taste of home, this book provides plenty of options. Here are a few ideas for when you're hungry for . . .

Something Healthy: Start your day off with Strawberry Almond Overnight Oats (page 39) or a satisfying Apple Cranberry Yogurt Salad (page 68). Pack up some Shawarma Roasted Chickpeas (page 61) for an on-the-go snack.

Something Meatless: Fill up with a Veggie Gyro (page 73) or a Vegetarian Burrito Bowl (page 86). Try a Mocha Smoothie (page 37) to get you through an all-night study session.

Something Crunchy: Snack on crispy Everything Bagel Potato Chips (page 48) or Microwave Kettle Corn (page 57). For something more substantial, whip up some Crispy Oven "Fried" Chicken (page 108) for dinner.

Something Sweet: Satisfy your sweet tooth with Banana Bread in a Mug (page 122) or try dipping crispy Cinnamon Tortilla Crisps (page 50) into Pineapple Salsa (page 54).

Something Comforting: Classics like Microwave Mac & Cheese (page 91) and Microwave Spaghetti Marinara (page 104) will remind you of home, while a Microwave Chocolate Chip Cookie (page 120) is pure comfort food.

Something Fast and Flavorful: Creamy Fettuccine Alfredo (page 105) and Microwave Chicken Enchiladas (page 92) are full of flavor and ready in less than 15 minutes. Top it off with 5-Minute Apple Crisp (page 123).

Something Fancy-ish: Impress your friends with Ravioli Lasagna (page 106), Miso-Glazed Salmon (page 116), or Brown Sugar Garlic Pork Medallions (page 112).

8 Simple Steps to Becoming an Awesome Cook

The key to becoming a good cook is to master the basics. Skills like using basic tools, prepping ingredients, seasoning food, and learning to tell when food is cooked through are essential for successful cooking. Even if you have little to no cooking experience, learning these fundamentals will put you on the right path to developing your cooking chops.

1. **Have the right equipment:** Take stock of the cooking tools and ingredients that you have on hand. Decide what other tools you need to pick up to stock your college kitchen (see page 6 for more details).

2. **Make a list of recipes you want to try:** Keep a running list of recipes that you want to try. Look for recipes that use equipment and ingredients available to you. If storage space is an issue, look for recipes that can be adapted for single servings.

3. **Try new flavors and ingredients:** Cooking for yourself is a great way to expand your palate and try different seasonings or ingredients. This is also a great time to explore different flavor combinations from other cultures that interest you.

4. **Watch your favorite cooking show:** There are so many fun and entertaining celebrity chefs to watch and stream. You can learn valuable skills, new flavor combinations, and so much more.

5. **Follow the recipe:** When trying a new recipe, be sure to follow the directions as written. Recipes, especially for baked goods, are often written with precise measurements and instructions for a reason. If you'd like to try a variation, take notes on changes you'd like to make. Once you feel comfortable making the recipe as it's written, feel free to test your variations.

6. **Practice your skills:** Set aside time for cooking each week. As with most things, practice makes perfect when it comes to cooking. The more time you spend practicing your skills, the better you will become.

7. **Track your progress:** Take plenty of photos of your creations. Not only is it Insta-fun, but you'll also have a visual record of how far you've come.

8. **Cook with a friend:** Cooking is always more fun with a friend. Grab your bestie, turn up your favorite playlist, and hang out in the kitchen. Not only will you end up with great food to enjoy together, but you'll make some lifelong memories along the way.

SHOPPING WITHOUT BREAKING THE BANK

When you're just starting out, you may not have everything you need to make your favorite recipes. If your kitchen isn't fully stocked with the equipment, tools, and ingredients you need, don't worry. There are a number of ways you can stock your college kitchen on a tight budget.

First, check with family and friends—they might have spare items they are willing to give you. You can also ask for kitchen gear as gifts for holidays or birthdays. Another way to score affordable gadgets is by scouring local thrift shops, garage sales, or online sales.

There are some great deals to be had on kitchen gadget sets or bundles, such as utensils, measuring equipment, cookware, and bakeware. A word of caution when buying kitchen gadget sets, however: Make sure you will actually use all of the items in the set. Many times, there are items included that you'll never use.

When it comes to ingredients, you can usually find good deals with a little preparation. Plan your meals around your grocery store's weekly sale items. Most stores change their sale items each week, so watch for your favorites to go on sale. A great way to cut costs in half is to shop with a friend and buy items in bulk to share. Other ways to save on groceries include shopping at stores that offer student discounts and buying store-brand items.

Crucial Kitchen Gear

With limited space and a tight budget, you may not have access to all of the equipment and appliances in a traditional kitchen. You may need to invest in some kitchen essentials, but don't worry! The basic tools and equipment you'll need are easy to find and not very pricey, and they'll quickly pay for themselves. Alternatively, you can always check with your friends or your RA to see if they're willing to lend you what you need. College cooking is all about getting the most out of the equipment and appliances available to you.

ESSENTIAL TOOLS

These tools are easy to find, relatively inexpensive, and don't take up much storage space.

A good knife: A sharp knife is your best tool. If you can have only one, start with a chef's knife. It can handle most kitchen tasks.

Aluminum foil and parchment paper: You can use these for cooking and baking. You can also wrap food in them for storage.

Can opener: Look for a can opener with comfortable grips and a large turning knob.

Cutting board: A thick plastic cutting board provides a safe and solid surface for slicing and dicing that's also easy to clean. To figure out what size you need, place your knife diagonally across the board. The board should extend beyond both ends of the knife by at least one inch.

Food storage containers: A set of food storage containers with airtight lids is essential for storing leftovers. They can even serve double duty as small mixing bowls.

Measuring cups and spoons: There are three tools you'll need for measuring—a 2-cup wet measuring cup, a set of nested dry measuring cups, and a set of measuring spoons. Look for microwaveable ones made of glass or sturdy plastic.

Meat thermometer: Using a meat thermometer is the only way to accurately tell if meat is properly cooked.

Microwave-safe mug: A standard-size coffee mug is perfect for making many single-serve recipes in this book.

Mixing bowls: For college cooking, glass bowls are preferred because they can be used in the microwave. With both a 5-quart and a 3-quart bowl, you'll be able to handle any cooking task.

Potholders or an oven mitt: Even if you only have access to a microwave, keep a set of sturdy potholders or an oven mitt handy to protect yourself from burns.

Pot with a lid: A 3-quart aluminum or stainless-steel saucepan or stockpot with a lid is the most versatile. Choose one with the thickest base you can afford.

Rimmed baking sheet: A baking sheet that is at least 15½ inches by 10 inches is perfect for baking and roasting in an oven.

Skillet or frying pan: A 10-inch aluminum or stainless-steel skillet or frying pan will get most jobs done. Choose one with the thickest base you can afford.

Spatulas: You'll need two types of spatulas: a 12-inch scraper spatula with a silicone head for mixing and a nylon or plastic slotted turning spatula for tasks like flipping eggs.

Tongs: Sturdy, 12-inch kitchen tongs with silicone tips are useful for transferring ingredients into or out of hot pans as well as mixing and serving salads and pastas.

Whisk: A metal or silicone whisk is a handy tool for mixing ingredients together.

ESSENTIAL EQUIPMENT

Here are a few pieces of equipment you might consider investing in. Before buying a hot plate or toaster oven for a dorm room, check with your college to make sure they're allowed.

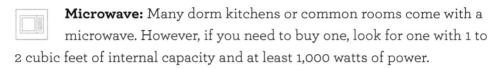 **Microwave:** Many dorm kitchens or common rooms come with a microwave. However, if you need to buy one, look for one with 1 to 2 cubic feet of internal capacity and at least 1,000 watts of power.

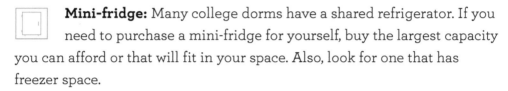 **Mini-fridge:** Many college dorms have a shared refrigerator. If you need to purchase a mini-fridge for yourself, buy the largest capacity you can afford or that will fit in your space. Also, look for one that has freezer space.

 **Blender:** A blender is great for making smoothies, dressings, and dips. There are many versions available, but the single-serving type is a great space-saving option for dorm rooms.

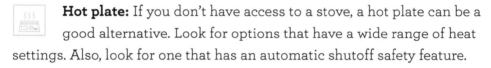 **Hot plate:** If you don't have access to a stove, a hot plate can be a good alternative. Look for options that have a wide range of heat settings. Also, look for one that has an automatic shutoff safety feature.

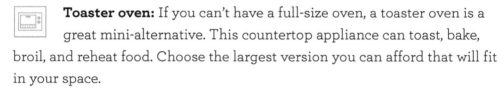 **Toaster oven:** If you can't have a full-size oven, a toaster oven is a great mini-alternative. This countertop appliance can toast, bake, broil, and reheat food. Choose the largest version you can afford that will fit in your space.

WHAT DOES THAT WORD MEAN AGAIN?

Cooking can be intimidating because it has its own language. Understanding common cooking terms can help make it easier for you.

Preheat: Turning on an oven to a specified temperature or applying heat to a pan before adding any ingredients. When the oven reaches the given temperature or when the pan is hot, you can begin cooking.

Simmer: Cooking a liquid at just below the boiling point. Small bubbles will form around the edges of the liquid.

Boil: Cooking a liquid to the point of bubbling (around 212°F). Larger bubbles will form and will break through the surface of the cooking liquid.

Sauté: Putting fat into a hot pan, heating it up, then adding the ingredients and moving them around in the pan while they cook.

Sear: Cooking food, usually meat, in a hot pan at a high temperature until a brown crust forms on the outside.

To taste: Adding salt, pepper, or seasonings to bring the flavor of the dish to your liking.

Slice: Cutting ingredients into flat pieces of roughly the same size and thickness.

Whisk: Beating ingredients with a fork or a whisk to combine them and incorporate air.

Chop: Cutting food into smaller pieces (all roughly the same size) so they will cook faster and more evenly.

Dice: Cutting food into small cubes, usually ⅛ to ¼ inch.

Mince: Cutting food into tiny pieces.

Dredge: Coating food in a dry ingredient, such as bread crumbs or flour, to form a crust when cooked, such as the chicken in Crispy Oven "Fried" Chicken (page 108).

Transfer: To move food from one vessel to another, such as from a pan to a plate, or from one heat source to another, such as from the stove to the oven.

Stand or rest: Allowing food to sit or cool at room temperature for a period of time.

Divided: Separating an ingredient so that it can be used in more than one step in a recipe.

Must-Have Ingredients

One of the keys to becoming a great college cook is having basic ingredients on hand. Here are some inexpensive and easy-to-find ingredients to keep in your kitchen that you can easily pull together to make a satisfying meal from the recipes in this book.

PANTRY

All-purpose flour: All-purpose flour is the basis for many baked goods. It's also used as a coating for meats or a sauce thickener. Store flour in an air-tight container in a cool, dark place or refrigerate it, if you have the space.

Bread: Bread is a versatile ingredient that can be used in a variety of recipes in this book. The recipes in this book use white sandwich bread, unless otherwise noted. However, you can easily substitute your favorite type of bread.

Canned goods: Canned items have a long shelf life and are simple to prepare. You can whip up a healthy meal in no time with canned beans, vegetables, tuna, or chicken. Canned beans and meats can be added to many recipes for extra protein.

Grains: Grains, such as rice, oats, and quinoa, can be stored at room temperature for long periods of time. Keep your grains tightly sealed and away from moisture.

Jarred sauces: Marinara, Alfredo, enchilada, and pesto sauces can add great flavor to many recipes. Once open, unused sauce can be stored in the refrigerator for up to one week. Some sauces can even be frozen for up to 3 months.

Nut butters: Your favorite nut butter can satisfy a sweet tooth and provide added protein to recipes. Depending on the type of nut butter, you may need to store it in the refrigerator once it's been opened.

Oil: Many recipes use oil, either as a recipe base or to help browning and prevent sticking. Canola, olive, or coconut oil can be used in the recipes in this book.

Pasta: If stored in an airtight container, such as a zip-top bag, in a cool, dry place, dried pasta has a long shelf life.

Seasonings: Salt and pepper are the most common seasonings to have on hand and are used throughout the recipes in this book. I also like to keep garlic powder, onion powder, and cinnamon on hand for flavor boosts.

Stocks: Chicken, beef, and vegetable stocks add great flavor to recipes. Freeze leftover stock in ice-cube trays, then transfer the frozen cubes to zip-top bags, where you can keep it for up to 6 months. You can use the frozen stock cubes in many recipes.

FRIDGE

Butter: Butter adds great flavor to recipes. The recipes in this book use unsalted butter, unless otherwise noted.

Cheese: Whether on its own or as part of another dish, cheese is a classic kitchen staple. You can buy cheese in a block and shred it yourself or save time and use the pre-shredded varieties.

Eggs: Eggs are a protein-rich staple that can be prepared in a number of ways. Eggs are also used in baking to provide structure and richness.

Fruit: Fresh (or frozen) fruits are a great way to satisfy a sweet tooth. You can also use them in dessert recipes or add them to salads. Apples, citrus fruit, and bananas all keep very well for at least a week and sometimes as long as two weeks.

Leafy greens: Leafy greens are great in salads, but they can also be used in sandwiches, pasta dishes, and soups.

Milk: Keep your favorite milk on hand for smoothies, oatmeal, baking, and more. You can use whole, low-fat, skim, or nondairy varieties.

Minced garlic: Garlic can add a lot of flavor to recipes. Using the jarred minced garlic is a great way to get added flavor without the fuss of peeling and chopping.

Vegetables: Fresh vegetables are a great way to round out a meal or to enjoy as a crunchy snack. Most vegetables are simple and easy to prepare. Carrots, broccoli, potatoes, and onions will last a few weeks when stored properly.

HOW TO USE LEFTOVERS FROM THE DINING HALL

If you can't get to the grocery store or if you only need a small amount of a certain ingredient, the dining hall can be a great resource. Pack an extra zip-top bag (or two) in your backpack to transport ingredients. Note that not all meal plans allow taking food out of the dining halls— so use your best judgment!

Bread: Need a slice of bread for BLT Avocado Toast (page 42)? Grab an extra from the dining hall.

Sliced Cheese: Snag an extra slice or two of cheese for the Ultimate Roast Beef Sandwich (page 80) or to top the Perfect Burger (page 95).

Salad Greens and Vegetables: Hit the dining hall salad bar for some salad greens to round out a Turkey Club Wrap (page 75) or top your Vegetarian Burrito Bowl (page 86). Grab some raw vegetables to use in Veggie Ramen (page 88) or to dip into Two-Ingredient Veggie Dip (page 51).

Fruit: Snag a spare banana or apple to use in Apple Cranberry Yogurt Salad (page 68) or for Banana Granola Bites (page 60).

Condiments: Don't forget the condiments. Packets of ketchup, mustard, mayonnaise, salad dressings, and sour cream can be used on sandwiches and salads.

How Long Food Lasts

Pantry items can last for quite a while before they spoil, but fresh foods, like produce, meat, and dairy, have a much shorter life span. Many packaged foods will tell you when the item should be sold or used by. But the terminology can be confusing, and for many foods, these dates are suggestions and do not necessarily mean the food is spoiled or unsafe.

When a package lists a "best by" date, it's more about taste than food safety. The "best by" date means that the product will have the best flavor and texture when used by the date printed on the label. If you see a "sell by" date on a package, this means that the seller should remove the item from the store shelves by the date printed on the label. However, the product is still safe to consume 5 to 7 days beyond this date, if stored properly. A "use by" date is the date the product is guaranteed to be fresh and of the best quality.

Unpackaged foods, such as fruits and vegetables, don't have labels and their freshness can be harder to determine. The length of time fruits and vegetables will remain fresh depends on the variety and how they are stored. Instead of washing produce all at once, wash it as you use it to extend its shelf life. To help prolong the freshness of greens, place a paper towel on top of the greens to absorb excess moisture.

Proper storage will ensure you can store your food for the maximum time. Open pantry items should be stored in airtight containers or in zip-top bags. Always try to remove as much air as possible before sealing.

Where you store your food also plays a role in freshness. While it may be convenient to store milk and other dairy items on the refrigerator door, they will actually last longer if stored toward the back of your refrigerator, where it is the coldest. Meats should be stored on the bottom shelf. Lastly, never store onions and potatoes together. The gases they emit will cause them to spoil faster.

MENU PLANNING MAGIC

Menu planning is one of the best time- and money-saving hacks. The process is simple. Jot down what you want to eat for each meal throughout the week. Start by taking stock of what ingredients you have on hand, then check what your local grocery store has on sale for the week. Consider your schedule, too. Do you need a grab-and-go dinner on the nights you have study group or during finals week? Or, is a friend's birthday coming up and you want to make something special?

Menu planning also helps minimize food waste. Use fresh ingredients with a shorter shelf life first. Also, consider buying items you can use in multiple meals. Here are some more suggestions to help you master menu planning.

Rotisserie Chicken: Rotisserie chicken makes a great dinner on its own, but leftovers can also be used in many recipes, such as Microwave Chicken Enchiladas (page 92) or as added protein on Sesame Ramen Salad (page 70).

Salad Greens: Greens tend to spoil fast, so it's best to use them quickly. Recipes like Cobb Salad Pitas (page 77) and Strawberry Pecan Quinoa Salad (page 66) are great ways to make use of packaged salad greens.

Black Beans: Stores regularly offer discounts on canned beans, and this is a great time to stock up. Canned black beans can be used in Southwest Black Bean Soup (page 99), Vegetarian Burrito Bowl (page 86), and as a topping on Bean and Cheese Quesadillas (page 85).

Apples: Apples are less expensive when you purchase them by the bag. Use them in Warm Apple Pie Dip (page 52) or 5-Minute Apple Crisp (Page 123).

Putting It All Together

As you can see, with a few key tools, some basic equipment, essential pantry items, and a little planning, you are well on your way to mastering college cooking. As with most things, the more you practice, the better you will become. One of the best ways to hone your skills is to set aside time to cook and practice your cooking techniques every day, or at least a few times each week.

The next chapter explains essential cooking techniques every college cook needs to know. You will learn tips and tricks for building flavor, being efficient in the kitchen, and making the most of your tools and equipment.

As you begin to learn different techniques and experiment with new flavors, you will notice your kitchen confidence starting to grow.

You've got this!

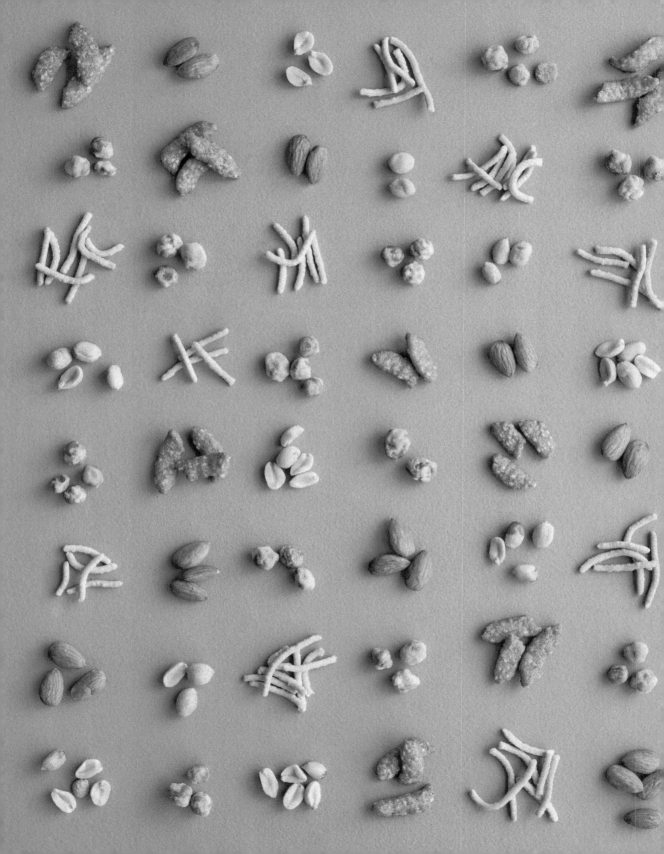

CHAPTER 2

COOKING 101

In this chapter, you'll learn the nuts and bolts of how to master cooking in your college dorm or small kitchen. You'll also learn the essential skills that every budding cook needs to know, including handling a knife, correctly measuring ingredients, and reading a recipe.

How to Prep

Success in the kitchen depends on how prepared you are. Once you start cooking, things can move quickly. It's important that you invest the time, up front, to prep as much as possible.

First, set up your workstation. Make sure your workspace is clean and that you have enough space. When working in a shared kitchen, you may need to find an area that is away from others. If you're cooking in your dorm room, you may need to get creative, such as converting your desk into a prep space.

Read through your recipe and gather any equipment you will need. Pull out the ingredients you will be using, except for raw meat—leave that in the refrigerator until you're ready to use it.

The final step is to prep your ingredients by washing, peeling, and chopping produce, grating cheese, and opening cans and packages. I also like to arrange my ingredients in the order that they will be used in the recipe.

RECIPES DECODED

Always read the entire recipe at least two times before you start cooking. Make sure you have the ingredients, tools, and time (including prep time, cook time, and cooling time) to prepare the recipe. Also, before you begin, look up any cooking terms you're not familiar with.

Title: This is the name of the recipe.

Prep Time: This includes the time it takes to prepare the ingredients before cooking, including chopping, measuring, and mixing.

Cook Time: This is the time it takes to cook or bake a recipe. Sometimes, you will need to stir or check on the food you are cooking. Other times, you can do something else while the food is cooking.

Headnote: This is an introduction or brief explanation of the recipe. You may also find additional details about the recipe like flavor, texture, or serving suggestions.

Yield: The number of servings the recipe makes.

Ingredient List: This is a list of all of the ingredients in the recipe along with the exact amount needed. Ingredients are listed in the order they are used in the recipe. When reading the ingredient list, you may notice that some ingredients have a comma with extra instructions. If a recipe ingredient has a comma after it, the instruction after the comma should be completed after the ingredient is measured. For example, "1 cup walnuts, chopped" means you measure one cup of walnuts and then chop them.

Directions: Step-by-step explanation of how to prepare the recipe. Always follow the directions in the order in which they are listed.

How to Measure

Many recipes require precise ingredient measurements. This is especially true when it comes to baked goods. To make sure your recipe turns out great, you'll need to know how to measure different ingredients the right way.

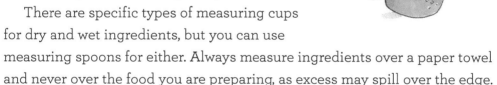

There are specific types of measuring cups for dry and wet ingredients, but you can use measuring spoons for either. Always measure ingredients over a paper towel and never over the food you are preparing, as excess may spill over the edge.

DRY INGREDIENTS

When measuring dry ingredients, use an individual measuring cup specifically for that measurement. Dry measuring cups are sold in sets that usually include 1 cup, ½ cup, ⅓ cup, and ¼ cup. Begin by spooning ingredients into the cup and then using a straight edge, such as a knife, to level off any excess.

WET INGREDIENTS

Liquid ingredients should be measured in transparent measuring cups with graduated measurements printed on them and a spout for easy pouring. Always measure wet ingredients by placing your measuring cup on a flat surface and pouring the ingredient into it. With the measuring cup still on the flat surface, read the measurement at eye level.

How to Mix

You will notice that various recipes involve different types of mixing. Mixing refers to combining ingredients. The method for mixing and the tools used vary based on the mixing type.

STIR

Stirring is a method used to thoroughly combine ingredients. Use a spoon or scraper spatula to mix the ingredients in a circular motion.

If a recipe says, "Be careful not to overmix," it means you should stir the ingredients until they are just combined. Do not continue to stir the ingredients beyond this point, as it will make the finished product tough.

FOLD

Folding is a method used when you need to incorporate delicate ingredients into denser ingredients, like whipped cream into a thick batter, or to evenly distribute pieces of fruit, nuts, or chocolate throughout a dough or batter. Use a spoon or scraper spatula to cut down the middle of the batter and gently fold

it over into the other half. Repeat this process until the ingredients are fully combined without streaks.

WHISK

Whisking is a method used to vigorously mix ingredients together until fully combined or to incorporate air into the mixture, as with whipped cream or egg whites, to make them light and fluffy. Whisking is also used for emulsifying, or combining ingredients that don't usually mix well, like oil and water or oil and vinegar. Whisking is usually done with a whisk, a fork, or electric beaters.

TOSS

Tossing is a method used to combine ingredients by lifting and dropping, such as with salads or pasta. This is usually done at the end of a recipe and is especially helpful when you want to coat ingredients in a sauce or dressing. Use tongs or a fork and spoon to toss.

How to Use a Knife

Learning how to properly use a knife is one of the most important cooking skills to develop. When you hold a knife properly, the knife will do the work for you. Proper knife skills will not only increase efficiency in the kitchen but also prevent injuries.

The most common kitchen knife is a chef's knife. Look for an 8- to 10-inch chef's knife within your budget. This might seem like a daunting size, but you may be surprised to learn that the bigger the blade, the safer it is to cut with!

You also want to make sure that your knife is sharp. Dull knives can slip when cutting. To ensure your knives stay sharp, always handwash your knives and don't put them in the dishwasher, as this will dull them.

HOW TO HOLD A KNIFE

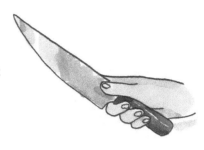

Balance the knife gently in the palm of your hand. Place your middle, ring, and pinky fingers around the handle with your middle finger close to the part where the handle meets the blade; this is known as the bolster. Place your index finger against the blade on the side (not the top), close to the handle. Place your thumb on the opposite side of the blade.

Use your free hand to hold the food you are cutting in place. Make sure your fingertips are curled under like a claw to prevent injury. Use this hand to gently guide the item you're cutting toward the blade.

Nearly every recipe calls for chopping, slicing, or dicing. When you're cutting a round item, like a potato or a carrot, cut it in half first. Then, place the flat side on the cutting board and begin cutting.

SLICE

Cut the item into thin, broad pieces. Your knife should go through the item in a single motion, not sawing back and forth.

CHOP

Cut the item into smaller, uniform pieces. Just like slicing, focus on chopping in a single motion, not sawing back and forth.

DICE

Cut the item into slices. Then, cut the slices into matchsticks. Finally, cut the matchsticks, crosswise, into small uniform cubes.

MINCE

Mincing is very similar to dicing, but the item is cut into much finer pieces. First, cut the item into thin slices. Then, cut the slices into thin matchsticks. Finally, cut the matchsticks crosswise into fine pieces. If the pieces still seem too large, use your knife to chop them even finer.

SAFETY FIRST

When it comes to cooking, safety should be your number one priority, even if you're making something as simple as a sandwich or a salad. Here are some safety guidelines you should always follow.

Wash Your Hands: Always wash your hands with soap and warm water before you start cooking and after handling raw meat or seafood, making sure to get in between your fingers and under your fingernails.

Keep Your Work Area Clean: Always start with a clean work area. Place dirty dishes in the sink as you go and clean up spills immediately. Always re-sanitize your work area after handling raw meat.

Wash Your Produce: Wash and dry all produce before you begin to prep. Even produce with skin needs to be washed before peeling to prevent cross contamination with the peeler.

Keep Meat, Fish, and Seafood Refrigerated: Keep raw meat, fish, and seafood in the refrigerator until you're ready to use it. Be sure to use a designated cutting board and knife when prepping meats, fish, and seafood to prevent cross contamination.

Practice Knife Safety: Always cut on a stable surface with a sharp knife. Don't get distracted when using a knife, and focus on precision and safety, not speed. If you drop your knife, let it fall. Never try to catch a falling knife.

Prevent Burns: Always turn pot and pan handles inward when cooking on a stove or hot plate. When removing pot lids, stand back and remove the lid away from your face so the steam doesn't hit you. Never use damp potholders on a hot handle, as you could get burned.

How to Season Food

One of the most important things you can do to ensure your food tastes great is to season it properly. Seasoning usually refers to adding salt, but it can also include adding pepper, acid, fat, spices, and herbs.

When you add your seasoning is just as important as what you add. For example, it's important to salt your food throughout the cooking process so that each layer is seasoned. When you spread out the salting throughout your cooking process, it enhances the natural flavors of the ingredients and brings them to life rather than making the food taste salty.

When a recipe calls for pepper, it usually means ground black pepper, unless otherwise noted. Like salt, ground black pepper enhances the flavor of food. However, you don't want to add pepper as often as you add salt. You'll end up with peppery food.

When adding dried herbs and spices, you want to make sure they have a chance to heat up. Many dried herbs and spices will taste much better if they have time to release their natural flavors into the dish. It's also important to make sure they haven't expired as they lose their flavor over time. Make a habit of checking expiration dates and discard any that are beyond their prime.

Fat and acid are other ways to brighten your dishes and make them taste better. A squirt of lemon juice or a splash of vinegar can give your dish a flavor boost. And, adding a pat of butter or a drizzle of olive oil can take a sauce from ho-hum to oh, yum!

When it comes to seasoning, always start by following the recipe instructions. As you become more experienced, you can get more adventurous with seasoning. Finally, don't be afraid to taste as you go (with the exception of cooking meat) and adjust the seasoning as needed. Trust your palate to make sure your food tastes good.

Cooking with a Microwave

Microwaves are the most common cooking appliance in dorms, and, in some cases, they may be the only cooking appliance allowed. The good news is, you can do a lot with a microwave, from boiling water and steaming vegetables to crisping bacon and melting butter and chocolate. In fact, many of the recipes in this book were designed specifically for the microwave.

Here are three basics that are easy to cook in a microwave.

Rice: Put ½ cup long-grain rice into a medium microwave-safe bowl (preferably glass). Add 1¼ cups water and a pinch of salt. Microwave on high for 6 minutes. Drape a kitchen towel over the bowl, leaving a ½-inch gap for steam to escape. Microwave on high for another 5 minutes. Allow the rice to sit in the microwave, covered, for 3 minutes. Fluff with a fork before eating.

Pasta: Put ½ cup pasta into a medium microwave-safe bowl and add enough water to cover the pasta by 1 to 2 inches. Add a pinch of salt. Place the bowl on top of a plate and microwave on high for the recommended cooking time on the package plus 3 to 4 minutes. Drain the pasta before serving.

Steamed vegetables: Cut the vegetables into uniform pieces and place them in a single layer in a medium microwave-safe bowl. Cover the bowl tightly with plastic wrap and cook on high for 30 to 45 seconds. Carefully cut a slit in the plastic wrap to allow steam to escape, then unwrap the bowl and serve.

When you're cooking meat and fish in a microwave, make sure the pieces are the same size and thickness, and remove any excess fat or large bones. This ensures the meat cooks evenly. Always check the internal temperature of meat and fish with a meat thermometer to make sure it is at the proper temperature before eating.

Even though there are many things you can make in a microwave, there are a few safety precautions to note. Do not cook frozen meats, processed lunch meats, hot peppers, carrots, or whole eggs in the microwave. Not only will they not cook properly, but hot peppers and carrots have been known to start fires. Also, do not put metal or aluminum foil in a microwave, as it can spark and start a fire.

Finally, because microwaves vary in power output from model to model, it's important to know the wattage of your microwave before you start cooking. In most cases, you can find the wattage of your microwave printed inside the microwave door. If not, you can look it up online by searching for the make and model. The recipes in this book are based on a 1500-watt microwave. Depending on the wattage of your microwave, you may need to increase or decrease the cooking time.

7 MIND-BLOWING MICROWAVE HACKS

You can use your microwave for so much more than reheating last night's takeout or nuking frozen burritos. Try these microwave hacks to make everyday cooking and cleanup easier.

1. **Easily Peel Garlic:** Microwave a whole head of garlic for 30 seconds. The cloves will easily pop out of the papery skin.

2. **Heating Bread and Tortillas:** Place a damp paper towel on top of the bread or tortillas. Microwave on LOW (30% power) for 30 seconds.

3. **Make Milk Foam:** You can skip the coffee shop with this hack. Simply shake milk in a jar with a lid for 30 seconds then pop it in the microwave for 30 seconds.

4. **Stop Crying When Cutting Onions:** Cut both ends off an onion and microwave it for 30 seconds before cutting—no more tears!

5. **Ripen an Avocado:** No more waiting for avocados to ripen. Pierce an unripe avocado with a fork, wrap it in a paper towel, and microwave it for 30 seconds.

6. **Sanitize a Kitchen Sponge:** Clean a germy kitchen sponge by soaking it in water and microwaving it on high for 1 minute. Allow the sponge to cool before handling it.

7. **Clean a Messy Microwave:** Put 1 cup water into a small microwave-safe bowl. Squeeze a lemon into the water, then cut the lemon and put the slices into the bowl. Cook on HIGH (100% power) for 3 to 4 minutes, or until the water boils. Leave the door closed and let the bowl sit for 5 minutes. Wipe down the inside of the microwave with a sponge or cloth.

Cooking with a Toaster Oven

Another college-friendly kitchen appliance is the toaster oven. Its functions go way beyond toasting bread. Today's toaster ovens are like mini versions of traditional ovens. Some colleges do not allow toaster ovens in dorm rooms (check with your RA); you may have access to this useful appliance in your common area.

You can bake things like cakes, cookies, and pies in a toaster oven. And, because they have a smaller capacity than traditional ovens, they're perfect for making small batches of your favorite recipes.

You can also use a toaster oven to roast meats, such as chicken, pork, and beef. And, you can make quick-cooking fish in foil packets for a lighter option. But the toaster oven isn't just for baked goods and meats. Round out your meal by making baked potatoes or easy roasted vegetables in the toaster oven. You can even reheat leftovers in it. Unlike in a microwave, the food will heat evenly and not get soggy.

Of course, you can heat up frozen foods in a toaster oven by following the package instructions. But did you know that you can also make crispy taco shells from a soft corn or flour tortilla? Move the rack to the upper third of the toaster oven. Evenly drape a soft tortilla over two rungs of the wire rack, and bake until the tortilla is golden brown and crispy.

Toaster ovens are also great for making snacks like granola, toasted nuts, or even s'mores. You can whip up a batch of toaster oven s'mores by placing graham cracker squares on a foil-lined baking sheet, then topping each one with a piece of chocolate and a marshmallow. Broil until the marshmallows turn golden. Remove the tray from the toaster oven and top each s'more with another graham cracker square.

Cooking with Pots, Pans, and Other Appliances

To create a delicious meal, you need the proper tools. Pots and pans are essential when cooking on a stove or a hot plate. You may also want to have a few other appliances to help make the job easier, such as a blender or an oven.

PANS

Pans are usually shallow cooking vessels with sides that extend an inch or so above the base, usually under three inches tall, and the sides slant outward slightly. Pans do not hold much liquid, which is what sets them apart from pots. The most common types of pans are frying pans and skillets, such as cast-iron skillets and electric skillets.

Pans are used for sautéing, searing, and frying. Sauté is French for "jump." When sautéing, you put butter or oil into a hot pan and then add your ingredients. You keep the food moving (or jumping) in the pan, so it maintains an even heat.

Searing, on the other hand, is the exact opposite. Like sautéing, you put a small amount of fat into a hot pan and then the food, but you let the food sit and don't move it around in the pan. You want the item, such as a piece of meat, to develop a golden crust before flipping it and searing the other side. You'll know when it's ready to flip because the meat will no longer stick to the pan.

Frying is when you cook food partially (or fully) submerged in hot fat, such as oil. Like searing, you allow the food to cook in the fat until it develops a crispy, golden crust before flipping it.

POTS

Pots, unlike pans, have deeper, straight sides, usually over four inches tall. Pots are typically used when cooking foods with liquid, as the taller sides allow for more even heat distribution. Pots also come with lids to help trap heat and steam so foods cook faster.

Pots are typically used for boiling, simmering, and steaming. Boiling is when liquid is heated to 212°F and is vigorously bubbling. Boiling is great for cooking pasta and blanching vegetables.

Simmering is when liquid is just below the boiling point and small bubbles start to form around the edge of the pot. Some of the bubbles may even start to pop through the surface of the liquid. Simmering is great for soups and sauces.

Steaming is a form of cooking in which you create moist heat by boiling water. Food is kept in a separate container within the pot, like a steamer basket, where it doesn't come into direct contact with the water. As the boiling water vaporizes, the steam gently cooks the food.

BLENDER

Blenders are tabletop kitchen appliances used for mixing, pureeing, and chopping food into small pieces. Blenders are the perfect tool for making smoothies, dressings, and soups. You can control the speed and amount of time food is processed in a blender. For chunkier textures, simply pulse the blender by turning it off and on in quick bursts. This is a great way to finely dice or mince foods.

OVEN

While smaller appliances, like toaster ovens and microwaves, are great for college cooking, some jobs require the power of an oven. Ovens are great for roasting and baking larger items that can't fit into a toaster oven. Ovens also have a large broiler, allowing larger quantities of food to be cooked.

Freestyling: Cooking Without a Recipe

While this book provides a wide variety of delicious recipes to satisfy any craving or mood, feel free to get creative! You might be inspired to make substitutions or change things up a bit using your new cooking know-how. Remember, take notes about what you changed so that you can recreate it if you love it. Below are some ways you can get creative in the kitchen.

Build a meal around a protein: Proteins, such as meats, fish, tofu, or legumes, make a great "base" for your dish. If you have leftovers of these ingredients, think about what grains, vegetables, or flavors might work well with them.

Swap out ingredients: If you love the flavors of a pork recipe but only have chicken on hand, swap out the pork for the chicken. Not a fan of a certain vegetable? Replace it with one you love.

Choose a cooking oil: Most of the recipes in this book use canola oil, but you can always use an equal amount of olive oil or coconut oil instead.

Use acid to bring out flavor: Adding an acidic ingredient is a great way to enhance a recipe. Try a squirt of lemon or lime juice or a splash of balsamic, white wine, or sherry vinegar. Each of these will add its own unique flavor, but you usually only need a small amount, otherwise your food may get too tart or bitter.

Look around for inspiration: Pay attention to the foods you eat at restaurants or in the dining hall. Note the flavors you like and how things are prepared. Scour cookbooks and blogs for recipes for similar dishes.

Experiment with different flavors: If there are certain flavors you love, such as lemon and pepper, try adding them to your favorite recipe. For example, you could add lemon pepper seasoning to steamed vegetables. Or, if you are not a fan of a certain flavor, like garlic, try replacing it with dried thyme or another herb. And, don't be afraid to step way outside the box—taco egg rolls, anyone?

The Recipes in This Book

All the recipes in this book were designed for a college kitchen setting. Whether you're in a dorm room or have a small kitchen, the recipes in this book are easy to prepare, and more than half of them can be made in a microwave or require no cooking at all. Most recipes are written for one person, but you can easily double or triple the ingredients to suit your needs.

I've included a mix of classic comfort foods (some with a modern twist) and lighter options for when you want to be more health conscious. They all feature the staple ingredients listed in chapter 1 and the cooking techniques covered in this chapter.

I've also used the following labels on the recipes to make it easy for you to do menu planning:

5 or Fewer Ingredients: dishes that contain fewer than 5 ingredients (excluding salt, pepper, water, and cooking spray)

15 Minutes: dishes that take less than 15 minutes from start to finish

Worth the Wait: anything that takes longer than 45 minutes to prepare

No Cook: recipes that don't involve any heating

Cheap Eat: recipes that cost less than $2 per serving, or about the price of a pizza slice

Healthy: dishes that are lighter

Vegetarian or **Vegan:** recipes that do not contain meat products (vegetarian), or recipes that use no animal products of any kind (vegan)

I've also labeled each recipe to indicate the cooking appliance used (microwave, toaster oven, blender, etc.), if any, and I've provided tips about how to adjust the recipes to suit different tastes, make them faster, or cook them using other pieces of equipment.

I'm so excited for you to get cooking!
Let's get started.

Microwave Scrambled Eggs, page 43

Microwave Bacon, page 44

CHAPTER 3

BREAKFAST

Chewy Chocolate Chip Granola Bars 36

Mocha Smoothie 37

Microwave Apple Cinnamon Oatmeal 38

Strawberry Almond Overnight Oats 39

Blueberry Pancake in a Mug 40

French Toast in a Mug 41

BLT Avocado Toast 42

Microwave Scrambled Eggs 43

Microwave Bacon 44

Sausage and Egg Breakfast Taquitos 45

Chewy Chocolate Chip Granola Bars

Makes 4 bars

Prep time: 5 minutes, plus 10 minutes to chill • **Cook time:** 2 minutes 30 seconds
Total time: 18 minutes

▢ Microwave

Cheap Eat, Vegetarian

Homemade granola bars are a quick and easy breakfast you can eat on the way to class, and they're also handy study snacks.

Nonstick cooking spray

2 tablespoons unsalted butter

2 tablespoons plus 2 teaspoons packed light brown sugar

2 tablespoons honey

Pinch salt

¼ teaspoon vanilla extract

1 cup quick oats

¾ cup crispy rice cereal

1½ tablespoons semi-sweet chocolate chips

1. Line a rimmed baking sheet with parchment paper or aluminum foil coated with nonstick cooking spray. Set aside.

2. Put the butter, brown sugar, and honey into a medium microwave-safe bowl. Microwave on HIGH (100% power) for 1 minute. Remove from the microwave and stir until combined. Microwave again on HIGH for 1 minute, 30 seconds. Remove the bowl from the microwave.

3. Stir in the salt and vanilla.

4. Carefully add the oats to the bowl and stir until fully combined. Fold in the crispy rice cereal and chocolate chips until they are evenly distributed and well-coated in the butter and sugar mixture.

5. Transfer the contents of the bowl to the prepared baking sheet and use your hands to firmly shape it into a 4-by-4-inch square.

6. Freeze for 10 minutes.

7. Remove the pan from the freezer and cut into bars.

8. Store leftovers in an airtight container at room temperature for up to 4 days.

Remix Tip: Swap out the chocolate chips for dried fruit, such as cranberries, cherries, or blueberries.

Mocha Smoothie

Makes 1 smoothie

Prep time: 5 minutes • **Total time:** 5 minutes

⬜ Blender   No Cook

15 Minutes, 5 or Fewer Ingredients, Cheap Eat, Vegetarian

Smoothies are one of my favorite go-to breakfasts because they take only minutes to make in a blender. This Mocha Smoothie is like having breakfast and coffee in one. You can easily change up the flavor of this smoothie by using flavored coffee or adding a sweetened flavored syrup instead of the honey or maple syrup. If you like your smoothies even frostier, add a few ice cubes in step 1.

1 frozen banana

1 cup strong coffee

1 tablespoon unsweet-
ened cocoa powder

½ cup plain Greek
yogurt

Honey or maple syrup

1. Put the banana, coffee, cocoa powder, and yogurt into a blender and blend until smooth.

2. Add honey to your desired sweetness.

3. Stir to combine, then pour into a glass and enjoy.

Make It Yourself: Don't have a coffee maker? Use instant coffee for this recipe. Fill a coffee mug with water and microwave it on HIGH (100% power) for 1 minute, 30 seconds. Remove the water from the microwave, add 1 teaspoon instant coffee granules, and stir until the coffee granules have completely dissolved.

Microwave Apple Cinnamon Oatmeal

Serves 1

Prep time: 5 minutes • **Cook time:** 6 minutes • **Total time:** 11 minutes

▢ Microwave

15 Minutes, Cheap Eat, Healthy, Vegetarian

Packed with flavor and ready in minutes, this easy microwave version of apple cinnamon oatmeal is a great way to start the day. Oats are a whole grain and a good source of vitamins and nutrients. And did I mention it's delicious?

½ **apple**

½ **tablespoon unsalted butter**

½ **cup old-fashioned rolled oats (not quick oats)**

1 **cup water**

1 **teaspoon vanilla extract**

¼ **teaspoon ground cinnamon**

2 **teaspoons brown sugar**

1. Remove the apple core and stem, then peel the apple. Dice the apple into small cubes.

2. Put the apple and butter into a microwave-safe bowl.

3. Microwave on HIGH (100% power) for 2 minutes, stirring after 1 minute.

4. Remove the bowl from the microwave and add the oats and water. Stir to combine.

5. Microwave on HIGH for 2 minutes, stirring every minute.

6. If you prefer more tender oats, continue to microwave on HIGH for up to 2 more minutes, stirring every minute.

7. Remove from the microwave and stir in the vanilla, cinnamon, and brown sugar.

Appliance Switch-Up: To make this recipe on a hot plate or stove, put the apples and butter into a small saucepan. Cover and cook over medium-high heat for 2 to 3 minutes. Add the oats and water to the saucepan and stir. Bring to a boil over medium-high heat. Reduce the heat to low and cook for 10 to 13 minutes, or until the desired tenderness is reached. Remove from the heat and stir in the vanilla, cinnamon, and brown sugar.

Strawberry Almond Overnight Oats

Serves 1

Prep time: 5 minutes, plus 8 hours or overnight to chill
Total time: 8 hours 5 minutes

No Cook

Cheap Eat, Healthy, Vegan, Worth the Wait

These overnight oats are a great breakfast option when you know you're going to have a busy morning, because you prepare them the night before. In this no-cook recipe, the oats soak up the milk overnight and become tender and ready to eat by morning. Feel free to use your favorite type of dairy or nondairy milk in this recipe.

½ cup strawberries

2 tablespoons slivered almonds

½ cup old-fashioned rolled oats

1 tablespoon brown sugar, plus more for topping

½ teaspoon chia seeds

½ teaspoon ground cinnamon, plus more for topping

1 cup almond milk

1. Remove and discard the stems from the strawberries, then cut the strawberries into small pieces.

2. Put the strawberries and almonds in a 16-ounce glass jar or medium bowl.

3. Add the oats, brown sugar, chia seeds, and cinnamon. Stir to combine.

4. Pour in the milk and stir, making sure the oats are completely submerged in the milk.

5. Cover the jar and refrigerate overnight.

6. Sprinkle additional brown sugar and cinnamon on top before eating.

Remix Tip: Try swapping the strawberries out for other fruit, such as blueberries, raspberries, diced apples, or raisins. You can also use chopped walnuts or pecans instead of almonds.

Blueberry Pancake in a Mug

Makes 1 mug pancake

Prep time: 5 minutes • **Cook time:** 2 minutes • **Total time:** 7 minutes

☐ Microwave

15 Minutes, 5 or Fewer Ingredients, Cheap Eat, Vegetarian

This Blueberry Pancake in a Mug is a twist on the classic griddle version without the wait. Because it's made in the microwave, it takes only minutes to make. The pancake cooks up light and tender, and the blueberries add a fresh pop of sweetness.

1 tablespoon unsalted butter

3 tablespoons water

⅓ cup pancake mix

2 tablespoons blueberries

Maple syrup, for serving

1. Put the butter into a small microwave-safe mug or bowl and melt it in the microwave on HIGH (100% power) for 45 seconds.

2. Add the water and pancake mix and stir until combined. The mixture will be lumpy.

3. Gently fold in the blueberries.

4. Microwave on MEDIUM (50% power) for 1 to 2 minutes, then check for doneness by inserting a toothpick into the center of the pancake. If the toothpick comes out clean, the pancake is done.

5. Serve with maple syrup.

Remix Tip: Make it a Banana Walnut Mug Pancake by replacing the blueberries in step 3 with 2 tablespoons of diced bananas and 1 tablespoon chopped walnuts. Follow the remaining steps as directed.

French Toast in a Mug

Makes 1 mug French toast

Prep time: 5 minutes • **Cook time:** 2 minutes • **Total time:** 7 minutes

▢ Microwave

15 Minutes, Cheap Eat, Vegetarian

French toast is one of my all-time favorite breakfasts, but it can be time consuming to make. This fast and easy microwave version is a great way to enjoy this breakfast classic without the fuss. The eggs, milk, cinnamon, and vanilla form a rich custard that soaks into the bread. When it cooks, the bread becomes tender, and the top gets a little crispy. You can take it over the top by adding berries.

1 bread slice

1 egg

2 tablespoons milk

¼ teaspoon ground cinnamon

½ teaspoon vanilla extract

Maple syrup, for serving

1. Cut the bread into cubes. Set aside.

2. In a small bowl, whisk together the egg, milk, cinnamon, and vanilla.

3. Put the cubed bread into an 8-ounce microwave-safe mug.

4. Pour the egg mixture over the bread and stir to combine.

5. Microwave on HIGH (100% power) for 1 minute, 30 seconds, or until the French toast is cooked through.

6. Serve with maple syrup.

Smart Shopping Tip: This recipe is great for using up stale bread, because the egg and milk mixture will soak into the bread to soften it. Often, grocery stores will sell their day-old breads for a discount. Scour the grocery store bakery for day-old breads or rolls and use them for this French toast. Cinnamon raisin bread, challah, and brioche are other delicious options.

BLT Avocado Toast

Makes 2 slices of toast

Prep time: 5 minutes • **Cook time:** 2 minutes • **Total time:** 7 minutes

⊡ Toaster Oven

15 Minutes, 5 or Fewer Ingredients

This BLT Avocado Toast is a mash-up of two of my favorites. Avocado toast is topped with classic BLT ingredients for a delicious, hearty breakfast or an easy lunch that's ready in minutes. The salty, crispy bacon is the perfect match for creamy avocado. If you have extra time, you can take this open-faced sandwich to the next level by putting a sunny-side-up egg on top!

2 slices of your favorite bread

1 large, ripe avocado

¼ teaspoon salt

Pinch ground black pepper

2 iceberg lettuce leaves

3 slices Microwave Bacon (page 44)

4 slices tomato

1. Place the bread slices in the toaster oven and toast to your desired doneness.

2. While the bread is toasting, remove the flesh from the avocado and place it in a bowl with the salt and pepper. Mash the avocado with a fork to your desired consistency.

3. Spread half of the mashed avocado onto each slice of toast.

4. Top each slice of toast with a lettuce leaf, 1½ slices of the bacon, and 2 tomato slices.

Make It Even Faster: Plan ahead for this recipe and use leftover bacon from another recipe. The next time you cook bacon, make an extra batch and store it in the refrigerator in an airtight container or zip-top bag for up to 4 days, so it's ready to use for this recipe.

Microwave Scrambled Eggs

Serves 1

Prep time: 5 minutes • **Cook time:** 2 minutes • **Total time:** 7 minutes

▢ **Microwave**

15 Minutes, 5 or Fewer Ingredients, Cheap Eat, Vegetarian

Scrambled eggs are a protein-rich breakfast that's perfect for days when you need extra brainpower. This fast and easy microwave version makes scrambled eggs a cinch. But if you want to make an over-easy egg instead, heat a microwave-safe plate in the microwave on HIGH (100% power) for 15 seconds. Spread 1 teaspoon of butter all over the warm plate, crack the egg in the center of the plate, and then microwave on HIGH for 45 seconds. Cook in 10-second increments until the egg reaches your desired doneness. Allow the egg to rest in the microwave for 30 seconds before eating.

1 teaspoon butter

3 large eggs

1 tablespoon whole milk

¼ teaspoon salt

Pinch ground
   black pepper

1. Put the butter in a small microwave-safe bowl and melt it in the microwave on HIGH (100% power) for 30 seconds.

2. Carefully swirl the melted butter around the bowl, making sure it covers the sides.

3. Crack the eggs into the buttered bowl.

4. Add the milk, salt, and pepper to the eggs and whisk until completely combined.

5. Microwave on HIGH for 45 seconds.

6. Carefully stir the eggs with a fork then microwave on HIGH for an additional 45 seconds, or until the eggs reach your desired consistency.

Remix Tip: Take your scrambled eggs to the next level. After step 5, add diced deli ham, crumbled Microwave Bacon (page 44), or shredded cheese to the eggs, then continue with step 6 as instructed.

Microwave Bacon

Makes 4 slices

Prep time: 5 minutes • **Cook time:** 4 minutes • **Total time:** 9 minutes

⬜ Microwave

15 Minutes, 5 or Fewer Ingredients

Bacon is one of my all-time favorites, but it can be messy to cook on a stove. This microwave version eliminates the mess, and the bacon turns out crispy every time. Enjoy this with Blueberry Pancake in a Mug (page 40) or on top of BLT Avocado Toast (page 42).

4 slices bacon

1. Line a microwave-safe dinner plate with two layers of paper towels.

2. Place four slices of bacon on the paper towels without letting them touch.

3. Place two layers of paper towels on top of the bacon.

4. Microwave on HIGH (100% power) for 4 minutes.

5. Check the doneness of the bacon. If it's not crispy enough for your liking, continue cooking in 30-second increments until done.

6. Carefully remove the plate from the microwave and immediately remove all of the paper towels. If the bacon cools on the paper towels, it will stick to the paper.

Appliance Switch-Up: You can also make crispy bacon in a toaster oven. Line the toaster oven pan with aluminum foil. Arrange the bacon slices on the pan without letting them touch. Set the toaster oven to 400°F and bake for 12 to 15 minutes, or until the bacon reaches your desired crispness.

Sausage and Egg Breakfast Taquitos

Makes 2 taquitos

Prep time: 5 minutes • **Cook time:** 20 minutes • **Total time:** 25 minutes

Microwave Oven

5 or Fewer Ingredients

Flour tortillas are filled with sausage, eggs, and cheese and baked until crispy. You can easily double this recipe and store the leftovers in an airtight container in the refrigerator for another day. To reheat the leftovers, simply wrap them in a damp paper towel and microwave for 45 seconds.

Nonstick cooking spray

4 precooked, packaged
    sausage links

1 recipe Microwave
    Scrambled Eggs
    (3 eggs, scrambled)
    (page 43)

2 (6-inch) white corn
    tortillas or flour
    tortillas

2 tablespoons shredded
    cheddar cheese

1. Preheat the oven to 425°F. Spray a rimmed baking sheet with nonstick cooking spray.

2. Heat the sausage according to the package instructions and set aside.

3. Prepare the scrambled eggs.

4. Wrap the tortillas in a damp paper towel and microwave on HIGH (100% power) for 10 seconds.

5. Remove the tortillas and place them on the prepared baking sheet.

6. Place two sausage links, end to end, on each tortilla.

7. Place half of the scrambled eggs and half of the shredded cheese on each tortilla.

8. Tightly roll each tortilla and place it seam-side down on the baking sheet.

9. Bake for 10 to 15 minutes, or until the tortillas are crispy and the cheese has melted.

Remix Tip: Make vegetarian breakfast taquitos by swapping the sausage links for 2 tablespoons of cooked or steamed vegetables.

Spicy Wasabi Trail Mix, **page** 62

CHAPTER 4

SWEET AND SAVORY SNACKS

Everything Bagel Potato Chips 48

Cinnamon Tortilla Crisps 50

Two-Ingredient Veggie Dip 51

Warm Apple Pie Dip 52

Cookie Dough Dip 53

Pineapple Salsa 54

Classic Guacamole 55

Creamy Hummus 56

Microwave Kettle Corn 57

S'mores Caramel Popcorn 58

Microwave Granola 59

Banana Granola Bites 60

Shawarma Roasted Chickpeas 61

Spicy Wasabi Trail Mix 62

Mini Pepperoni Pizzas 63

Everything Bagel Potato Chips

Serves 2

Prep time: 5 minutes, plus 5 minutes to soak • **Cook time:** 9 minutes
Total time: 19 minutes

▢ Microwave

5 or Fewer Ingredients, Cheap Eat, Vegan

Did you know you can make potato chips in the microwave? You can easily swap out the everything bagel seasoning for your favorite seasoning blend.

1 medium russet potato, scrubbed

1 to 2 tablespoons olive oil

½ teaspoon salt

1 teaspoon everything bagel seasoning

Ice water

1. Place a piece of parchment paper on a microwave-safe plate.

2. Fill a large bowl halfway with ice and top with cold water until the bowl is almost full.

3. Cut the potatoes as thinly as you can, keeping the skin on. They should be almost transparent. Immediately submerge the potato slices in ice water. Allow them to soak for 5 minutes.

4. Remove enough potato slices from the ice water to cover the prepared microwave-safe plate in a single layer without touching. Dry the potato slices with paper towels and arrange them on the prepared plate. Leave the remaining potato slices in the ice water.

5. Brush the potato slices with a light coating of olive oil and sprinkle a pinch of salt over them.

6. Microwave on HIGH (100% power) for 2 minutes, 30 seconds.

7. Carefully remove the plate from the microwave and use tongs to flip the potato chips.

8. Return the potatoes to the microwave and cook on HIGH for another 2 minutes, or until golden brown.

9. Sprinkle lightly with the everything bagel seasoning while the chips are still warm.

10. Repeat steps 4 through 9 with the remaining potato slices.

Make It Yourself: Make your own everything bagel seasoning. In a small bowl, combine 2 tablespoons poppy seeds, 1 tablespoon white sesame seeds, 1 tablespoon black sesame seeds, 1 tablespoon plus 1 teaspoon dried minced garlic, 1 tablespoon plus 1 teaspoon dried minced onion, and 2 teaspoons sea salt. This recipe makes ½ cup of seasoning. Store in an airtight container at room temperature for up to 1 month.

Cinnamon Tortilla Crisps

Serves 2

Prep time: 5 minutes • **Cook time:** 7 minutes • **Total time:** 12 minutes

▭ Oven

15 Minutes, 5 or Fewer Ingredients, Cheap Eat, Vegan

These Cinnamon Tortilla Crisps are a sweet and crispy snack that's perfect for study sessions. They are baked in the oven, but you can easily make them in a toaster oven, too. Dip them into Pineapple Salsa (page 54) or Warm Apple Pie Dip (page 52).

4 (6-inch) flour tortillas

2 teaspoons canola oil

⅛ teaspoon ground cinnamon

2 teaspoons sugar

1. Preheat the oven to 400°F.

2. Cut each tortilla in half down the center and stack the halves on top of each other. Then, cut the stack in half down the center and cut each half in half again at an angle to form wedges. This will give you 8 wedges per tortilla.

3. Lay the wedges on a rimmed baking sheet and brush them with a light coating of canola oil. If you don't have a brush, you can dip a piece of paper towel into the oil and rub the oil onto each chip.

4. In a small bowl, mix together the cinnamon and sugar.

5. Sprinkle the cinnamon and sugar mixture on top of the chips.

6. Bake for 5 to 7 minutes, or until crispy.

Recipe Remix: To make a savory version of these crisps, replace the cinnamon and sugar with ½ teaspoon salt, ½ teaspoon ground black pepper, ½ teaspoon garlic powder, and ½ teaspoon onion powder. Combine the seasonings in a bowl and sprinkle over the chips in step 5.

Two-Ingredient Veggie Dip

Serves 2

Prep time: 5 minutes, plus 30 minutes to chill • **Total time:** 35 minutes

No Cook

5 or Fewer Ingredients, Cheap Eat, Vegetarian

This is my go-to dip for vegetables. It's super easy to make and can easily be doubled or tripled if you're getting together with friends. The flavor of this dip gets better the longer it sits. If you can, prepare it the day before and store it in an airtight container in the refrigerator until you're ready to eat it with assorted raw vegetables for dipping.

⅔ **cup sour cream**

2 teaspoons Italian dressing mix, such as Good Seasons

Assorted vegetables, for dipping

1. In a small bowl, combine the sour cream and Italian dressing mix and mix well.

2. Allow to chill for at least 30 minutes before serving.

3. Serve with vegetables for dipping.

Smart Shopping Tip: Buy store-brand sour cream. You can also save money by freezing excess sour cream for a later use. Premeasure the sour cream into ⅓ cup portions into snack-size zip-top bags and remove any excess air before sealing. Thaw the frozen sour cream in the refrigerator overnight, then whisk it to bring the thawed sour cream back to its original consistency.

Warm Apple Pie Dip

Serves 2

Prep time: 5 minutes • **Cook time:** 7 minutes • **Total time:** 12 minutes

▢ Microwave

15 Minutes, 5 or Fewer Ingredients, Cheap Eat, Vegan

This Warm Apple Pie Dip is like eating the filling from an apple pie. The best part is it takes only minutes to make in the microwave. Serve it with Cinnamon Tortilla Crisps (page 50) or use it as a topping for yogurt or ice cream.

2 apples

1 tablespoon lemon juice

3 tablespoons brown sugar

¼ teaspoon ground cinnamon

⅛ teaspoon nutmeg

1 teaspoon cornstarch

1 teaspoon water

1. Remove the apple cores and stems, then peel the apples. Cut the apples into small dice.

2. In a medium microwave-safe bowl, combine the apples, lemon juice, brown sugar, cinnamon, and nutmeg.

3. Microwave on HIGH (100% power) for 5 minutes or until the apple mixture is bubbling and juice comes out of the apples.

4. In a small bowl, combine the cornstarch and water and stir until the cornstarch has dissolved.

5. Add the cornstarch mixture to the cooked apples and stir well.

6. Return the bowl to the microwave and cook on HIGH for 2 more minutes, or until the sauce thickens.

Smart Shopping Tip: Apples are less expensive when you buy them by the bag. Use them in this recipe or in Microwave Apple Cinnamon Oatmeal (page 38) or Apple Cranberry Yogurt Salad (page 68). Apples don't need to be refrigerated if you're planning to eat them within 3 to 4 days.

Cookie Dough Dip

Serves 2

Prep time: 10 minutes, plus 30 minutes to chill • **Total time:** 40 minutes

No Cook

Cheap Eat, Vegetarian

If you're hit with a sudden craving for sweets while studying or hanging out with friends, this no-cook Cookie Dough Dip is sure to please! It takes only a few minutes to whip up and can easily be doubled or tripled, as needed. The hardest thing will be waiting for it to chill before diving in. Try it with apple slices, strawberries, vanilla wafer cookies, or graham crackers.

2 tablespoons unsalted butter, at room temperature

¼ cup sugar

¼ cup milk

½ teaspoon vanilla extract

¼ cup flour

Pinch salt

2 tablespoons mini chocolate chips

1. In a small bowl, whisk together the butter and sugar for about 2 minutes, or until light and fluffy.

2. Add the milk and vanilla and whisk until combined.

3. Whisk in the flour and salt until fully combined.

4. Fold in the chocolate chips and chill for at least 30 minutes.

Smart Shopping Tip: Pure vanilla extract can be pricey. You can save money by buying imitation vanilla extract, but you may need to use double the amount of imitation vanilla to get the same vanilla flavor.

Pineapple Salsa

Serves 2

Prep time: 10 minutes, plus 30 minutes to chill • **Total time:** 40 minutes

No Cook

Cheap Eat, Healthy, Vegan

This no-cook sweet and savory concoction makes an amazing dip. Serve it with Cinnamon Tortilla Crisps (page 50) or use it as a topping for chicken or fish. This salsa gets better the longer it sits.

2 (8-ounce) cans pine-apple, slices, chunks, or tidbits

2 teaspoons finely chopped jalapeño (for less heat, remove the seeds and ribs)

2 tablespoons finely chopped onion

2 teaspoons brown sugar

¼ cup orange juice

Juice of ½ lime

1. Drain the pineapple and cut it into small dice.

2. Transfer the diced pineapple to a medium bowl.

3. Add the jalapeño, onion, brown sugar, orange juice, and lime juice to the pineapple. Stir until combined.

4. Cover and chill in the refrigerator for at least 30 minutes before serving.

Smart Shopping Tip: If you only need a small amount of an ingredient, such as jalapeños or onions, use the grocery store salad bar. You can purchase the exact amounts you need and won't have any ingredients left over.

Classic Guacamole

Serves 2

Prep time: 10 minutes, plus 1 hour to chill • **Total time:** 1 hour 10 minutes

No Cook

Cheap Eat, Healthy, Vegan, Worth the Wait

This Classic Guacamole highlights the flavor and texture of avocados. You can use it as a dip or as a condiment for Turkey Club Wraps (page 75) or as a topping for Vegetarian Burrito Bowls (page 86). To speed up the prep, you can use jarred minced garlic instead of fresh garlic. This no-cook recipe is easy to prepare but needs time to chill before serving. It's definitely worth the wait!

2 ripe avocados

1 teaspoon salt

Pinch cayenne

1 lime

2 Roma tomatoes

¼ cup diced red onion

1 teaspoon minced garlic

2 tablespoons chopped fresh cilantro

1. In a medium bowl, combine the avocado flesh, salt, and cayenne. Using a fork, mash the avocados until they reach your desired consistency.

2. Squeeze the juice from the lime into the bowl and stir.

3. Cut each tomato in half, removing the seeds and pulp from both halves with a spoon. Cut each tomato into small dice. Add the tomato to the avocado mixture.

4. Add the onion, garlic, and cilantro and stir to combine.

5. Place a layer of plastic wrap on top of the guacamole, gently pressing it directly on top of the mixture to prevent browning.

6. Refrigerate for 1 hour before serving.

Make It Even Faster: Speed up the prep time of this recipe by using ¼ cup prepared pico de gallo from the grocery store deli section instead of the tomato, onion, garlic, and cilantro.

Creamy Hummus

Serves 2

Prep time: 10 minutes • **Total time:** 10 minutes

Blender   No Cook

15 Minutes, 5 or Fewer Ingredients, Cheap Eat, Healthy, Vegan

Hummus is a popular Middle Eastern dip that is creamy and flavorful. This hummus is free of gluten, nuts, and dairy, which makes it a great snack for everyone. Eat it as a dip with your favorite vegetables, crackers, or pretzels or use it as a spread on sandwiches and wraps, such as Veggie Gyros (page 73).

1 cup canned chickpeas (garbanzo beans), drained

¼ cup olive oil

1 tablespoon plus 1 teaspoon tahini

½ teaspoon lemon juice

½ teaspoon minced garlic

¼ teaspoon salt

Pinch ground black pepper

1. Put the chickpeas, olive oil, tahini, lemon juice, garlic, salt, and pepper into a blender. Blend to form a smooth paste. The longer you blend the hummus, the smoother it will become.

2. If the hummus is too thick, slowly drizzle in water while blending, until it reaches your desired consistency.

Make It Even Faster: Use jarred minced garlic instead of fresh garlic. If you want your hummus to have even more garlic flavor, use the oil in the jarred minced garlic in place of the olive oil in the recipe.

Microwave Kettle Corn

Serves 2

Prep time: 5 minutes • **Cook time:** 5 minutes • **Total time:** 10 minutes

☐ Microwave

15 Minutes, 5 or Fewer Ingredients, Cheap Eat, Vegetarian

If you like sweet and salty carnival-style kettle corn, you will love this easy microwave version. It's great when you want a quick snack for yourself, but you can also double or triple the recipe when you have friends over for a movie night.

1½ **teaspoons butter**

1½ **teaspoons canola oil**

1 **tablespoon brown sugar**

Pinch salt

3 **tablespoons popcorn kernels**

1. In a medium microwave-safe bowl, combine the butter, canola oil, brown sugar, and salt.

2. Microwave on HIGH (100% power) for 20 seconds, or until the butter is completely melted. Stir the mixture until it is fully combined.

3. Add the popcorn kernels to the butter mixture and stir to coat each kernel.

4. Spread the buttered kernels into a single layer in the bottom of the bowl.

5. Cover the bowl with plastic wrap and leave a ½-inch gap on one side as a vent.

6. Microwave on HIGH for 3 to 4 minutes. The popcorn is ready when you hear 1- to 2-second gaps between pops.

Remix Tip: Spice up your kettle corn by adding a pinch of ground cinnamon to the butter mixture before microwaving it. The cinnamon adds a warm layer of flavor to this sweet and salty snack.

S'mores Caramel Popcorn

Serves 2

Prep time: 5 minutes • **Cook time:** 30 seconds, plus 10 minutes to cool
Total time: 15 minutes

Microwave

15 Minutes, 5 or Fewer Ingredients, Cheap Eat

I created this recipe to use up leftover ingredients I had in my pantry. Enjoy this as an after-dinner treat or between classes.

½ **cup chocolate chips**

¼ **cup crushed graham cracker crumbs**

4 cups store-bought caramel popcorn (or 1 recipe Microwave Kettle Corn, page 57)

1 cup mini marshmallows

1. Line a rimmed baking sheet with parchment paper. Set aside.

2. Put the chocolate chips in a small microwave-safe bowl and microwave on HIGH (100% power) for 30 seconds. Remove from the microwave and stir.

3. Continue to microwave on HIGH in 10-second increments, stirring in between, until all of the chocolate chips have melted.

4. Pour the melted chocolate onto the parchment paper–lined baking sheet and spread it into a thin layer.

5. Sprinkle the graham cracker crumbs on top of the chocolate and then add the popcorn.

6. Lightly press on the mixture to ensure the popcorn adheres to the chocolate.

7. Allow to cool for at least 10 minutes so the chocolate hardens.

8. Break the chocolate-popcorn mixture into pieces and transfer to a large bowl.

9. Toss with mini marshmallows.

Make It Even Faster: Mix 4 cups of caramel popcorn with 2 cups of store-bought s'mores cereal.

Microwave Granola

Serves 2

Prep time: 5 minutes • **Cook time:** 4 minutes, plus 5 minutes to cool
Total time: 14 minutes

🔲 **Microwave**

15 Minutes, 5 or Fewer Ingredients, Cheap Eat, Healthy, Vegan

Granola is one of my favorite snacks, but the oven version can take over an hour to make. This fast microwave version has all of the same flavors and textures but only takes a fraction of the time to make. Mix up the flavor by swapping in different dried fruits, like dried cranberries or blueberries, or shredded coconut for the raisins. This granola is great on its own, as a yogurt topping, or in Banana Granola Bites (page 60).

2 tablespoons maple
syrup

1½ tablespoons water

4 teaspoons canola oil

¼ teaspoon salt

⅔ cup quick oats or
old-fashioned
rolled oats

2 tablespoons chopped
nuts or seeds of
your choice

2 tablespoons raisins

1. In a medium microwave-safe bowl, combine the maple syrup, water, canola oil, salt, oats, and nuts and stir.

2. Microwave on MEDIUM (50% power) for 2 minutes. Stir the mixture and microwave on MEDIUM for an additional 1 to 2 minutes, or until the oats have started to brown.

3. Remove from the microwave and stir in the raisins.

4. Allow the granola to cool for 5 minutes before eating.

Smart Shopping Tip: Head to the grocery store bulk bins to pick up nuts, seeds, and dried fruits. You can purchase the exact amounts you need so you don't have any leftovers.

Banana Granola Bites

Serves 2

Prep time: 5 minutes, plus 10 minutes to chill • **Cook time:** 15 seconds
Total time: 15 minutes

▢ Microwave

15 Minutes, 5 or Fewer Ingredients, Cheap Eat, Healthy, Vegetarian

When you're in the mood for a sweet but healthy snack, whip up a batch of these Banana Granola Bites. Peanut butter and banana are a classic combination that, when paired with granola, can be incredibly satisfying. You can easily turn this snack into a quick on-the-go lunch by wrapping the Banana Granola Bites in a whole-grain tortilla.

2 bananas

½ cup peanut butter

1 cup Microwave Granola (page 59)

2 teaspoons honey

1. Peel and slice each banana into 6 pieces.

2. Put the peanut butter in a small microwave-safe bowl and microwave it on HIGH (100% power) for 15 seconds, or until the peanut butter thins out.

3. Put the granola into a small bowl.

4. Dip one piece of banana into the melted peanut butter, making sure to coat all sides.

5. Roll the peanut butter–covered banana into the granola, making sure to lightly press the granola into the peanut butter. Place the coated banana on a plate. Repeat with the remaining banana pieces.

6. Refrigerate the coated bananas for 10 minutes.

7. Drizzle honey over the banana bites before serving.

Remix Tip: You can use any type of nut butter in this recipe. You can also make a chocolate version by using chocolate hazelnut spread instead of the peanut butter.

Shawarma Roasted Chickpeas

Serves 2

Prep time: 5 minutes • **Cook time:** 40 minutes • **Total time:** 45 minutes

Oven

5 or Fewer Ingredients, Cheap Eat, Healthy, Vegan, Worth the Wait

Shawarma is a popular Arab street food that consists of seasoned meats served in a wrap or pita bread. For this recipe, chickpeas are coated in a store-bought shawarma seasoning blend and roasted until crispy. These make a satisfying and crunchy snack on their own or a delicious topping for salads, like the Nutty Broccoli Salad (page 71).

1 cup canned chickpeas (garbanzo beans), drained

1 tablespoon olive oil

¼ teaspoon store-bought shawarma seasoning mix

Pinch salt

1. Preheat the oven to 450°F.

2. Pat the chickpeas dry with paper towels, then put them into a small bowl.

3. Add the olive oil, shawarma seasoning, and salt to the chickpeas. Stir until the chickpeas are completely coated in the mixture.

4. Spread the coated chickpeas in a single layer on a rimmed baking sheet.

5. Bake for 30 to 40 minutes, or until the chickpeas are golden and crunchy.

Remix Tip: These roasted chickpeas work great with other seasoning blends. Use leftover Italian seasoning from the Two-Ingredient Veggie Dip (page 51) or taco seasoning in place of the shawarma seasoning mix.

Spicy Wasabi Trail Mix

Serves 2

Prep time: 5 minutes • **Total time:** 5 minutes

No Cook

15 Minutes, 5 or Fewer Ingredients, Cheap Eat, Vegan

If you like spice, this crunchy Spicy Wasabi Trail Mix is for you. This no-cook recipe takes only minutes to pull together and uses only pantry ingredients. You can mix up a larger batch and store the extras in snack-size zip-top bags so you have a quick snack at the ready whenever you get a craving.

½ **cup peanuts**

½ **cup whole almonds**

½ **cup chow mein noodles**

¼ **cup dried wasabi peas**

½ **cup sesame sticks**

1. In a medium bowl, combine the peanuts, almonds, chow mein noodles, dried wasabi peas, and sesame sticks and stir well.

2. Store in an airtight container at room temperature for up to 4 days.

Remix Tip: For a less-spicy option, swap out the wasabi peas for the same amount of Shawarma Roasted Chickpeas (page 61).

Mini Pepperoni Pizzas

Serves 2

Prep time: 5 minutes • **Cook time:** 4 minutes • **Total time:** 9 minutes

🔲 Microwave 🔲 Toaster Oven

15 Minutes, 5 or Fewer Ingredients, Cheap Eat, Healthy

Nothing hits the spot quite like pizza! It's the perfect dorm room food—you can grab a slice anytime, and it tastes great even as leftovers. Easy, quick, and delicious, these Mini Pepperoni Pizzas will satisfy your pizza craving day or night. The best part is, they only take minutes to make in the microwave.

2 whole-grain English muffins

½ cup marinara sauce

16 slices turkey pepperoni

½ cup shredded mozzarella cheese

1. Split the English muffins in half and toast to your desired doneness.

2. Place the toasted English muffin halves, split-side up, on a microwave-safe plate.

3. Spread 2 tablespoons of marinara sauce on each English muffin half.

4. Arrange 4 slices of pepperoni on each English muffin half.

5. Top each half with 2 tablespoons of shredded mozzarella cheese.

6. Microwave on HIGH (100% power) for 1 to 2 minutes, or until the cheese has melted.

Appliance Switch-Up: These are just as easy to make entirely in the toaster oven, instead of the microwave. Preheat the toaster oven to 350°F while you prepare the pizzas as directed in steps 1 through 5, then bake for 6 minutes, or until the cheese has melted.

Brussel Sprouts Cranberry Salad, page 69

CHAPTER 5

QUICK SALADS AND SANDWICHES

Strawberry Pecan Quinoa Salad 66

Bacon and Blue Cheese Wedge Salad 67

Apple Cranberry Yogurt Salad 68

Brussels Sprouts Cranberry Salad 69

Sesame Ramen Salad 70

Nutty Broccoli Salad 71

Tuna Salad Avocado Bowls 72

Veggie Gyros 73

Lemon Pepper Tuna Lettuce Wraps 74

Turkey Club Wraps 75

Chicken Caesar Wraps 76

Cobb Salad Pitas 77

Caprese Chicken Grilled Cheese Sandwiches 78

Ultimate Roast Beef Sandwiches 80

Buffalo Chicken Flatbreads 81

Strawberry Pecan Quinoa Salad

Serves 1

Prep time: 10 minutes • **Total time:** 10 minutes

No Cook

15 Minutes, Healthy, Vegetarian

For this recipe you'll need cooked quinoa. I recommend cooking a batch of quinoa in the microwave (according to the package instructions) and keeping it in an airtight container in the refrigerator so you have it ready for a couple of quick lunches or dinners. Cooked quinoa will keep for up to 1 week. You can add extra protein to this salad by topping it with cooked chicken.

½ **cup spring mix salad**

1 **cup cooked quinoa**

¼ **cup chopped strawberries**

¼ **cup diced cucumber**

¼ **cup chopped pecans**

2 **tablespoons blue cheese crumbles**

2 **tablespoons balsamic vinaigrette salad dressing**

1. Place the spring mix salad in a serving bowl.

2. Microwave the quinoa according to the package instructions. Spoon the prepared quinoa in the center of the salad.

3. Arrange the strawberries, cucumber, pecans, and blue cheese around the quinoa.

4. Drizzle the salad dressing over the salad and toss to combine.

Make It Yourself: To make your own balsamic vinaigrette, in a small bowl, whisk together 1 tablespoon honey, 2 teaspoons Dijon mustard, ¼ teaspoon salt, ¼ teaspoon ground black pepper, ½ teaspoon minced garlic, and 2 tablespoons balsamic vinegar. Drizzle in ⅔ cup olive oil while whisking and continue to whisk until the dressing is emulsified. Refrigerate any unused vinaigrette in an airtight container for up to 1 week.

Bacon and Blue Cheese Wedge Salad

Serves 1

Prep time: 10 minutes • **Total time:** 10 minutes

No Cook

15 Minutes, 5 or Fewer Ingredients

Wedge salads get their name because the base is a quarter head of iceberg lettuce wedge that is topped with bacon and tomatoes and drizzled with blue cheese. You can take this over the top by adding your favorite salad fixings such as diced avocado, chopped hard-boiled egg, or chopped raw mushrooms. Serve it with The Perfect Burger (page 95) for the ultimate meal.

¼ **head iceberg lettuce**

¼ **cup blue cheese salad dressing**

1 **Roma tomato, chopped**

3 **slices Microwave Bacon (page 44), chopped**

2 **tablespoons blue cheese crumbles**

1. Place the lettuce on a serving plate.

2. Drizzle the salad dressing over the lettuce.

3. Top with the tomatoes, bacon, and blue cheese.

Make It Yourself: To make your own blue cheese salad dressing, in a small bowl, whisk together 2 tablespoons mayonnaise, 2 tablespoons sour cream, 2 tablespoons unsalted buttermilk, ½ teaspoon minced garlic, 1 teaspoon fresh lemon juice, ⅛ teaspoon salt, and a pinch of ground black pepper until combined and no longer lumpy. Fold in ¼ cup blue cheese crumbles. Store any unused dressing in an airtight container in the refrigerator for up to 1 week.

Apple Cranberry Yogurt Salad

Serves 1

Prep time: 5 minutes • **Total time:** 5 minutes

No Cook

15 Minutes, 5 or Fewer Ingredients, Healthy, Vegetarian

You can use any variety of apple that you have on hand in this salad. My favorite are Fuji apples because they're sweet, crisp, and juicy. Enjoy this salad for breakfast with a sprinkling of Microwave Granola (page 59) or as a sweet late-night study snack. Try drizzling some honey or add a dash of cinnamon for added flavor.

½ **apple, peeled, cored, and diced**

½ **cup seedless grapes, halved**

1 **tablespoon dried cranberries**

½ **tablespoon chopped walnuts**

½ **cup vanilla Greek yogurt**

1. In a medium bowl, combine the apple, grapes, cranberries, and walnuts.

2. Top with the yogurt and stir to combine.

Smart Shopping: Yogurt in single-serving containers is convenient but pricey. Buy yogurt in larger containers to reduce the price per serving.

Brussels Sprouts Cranberry Salad

Serves 1

Prep time: 10 minutes • **Total time:** 10 minutes

No Cook

15 Minutes, Healthy, Vegetarian

Brussels sprouts are leafy vegetables that resemble small cabbages. They are packed with nutrients and antioxidants. This is my favorite way to enjoy this nutritional powerhouse. Serve with Baked Chicken Tenders (page 94) for a complete meal.

8 to 10 medium Brussels sprouts

½ Granny Smith apple, cored and chopped

2 tablespoons dried cranberries

2 tablespoons chopped walnuts

2 tablespoons Vidalia onion vinaigrette salad dressing

2 tablespoons crumbled feta cheese

1. Cut the stem ends off the Brussels sprouts and peel away any leaves that are marked or wilted.

2. Cut the Brussels sprouts into very thin ribbons. Start by cutting a sprout in half lengthwise. Then place the sprout cut-side down and slice it crosswise into very thin shreds.

3. In a serving bowl, combine the shredded Brussels sprouts, apples, cranberries, and walnuts. Toss everything together until fully combined.

4. Drizzle the salad dressing over the salad, top with the feta cheese, and toss to combine.

Recipe Remix: You can easily substitute baby spinach for the Brussels sprouts. Use 2 cups of packed baby spinach that's been washed and dried thoroughly.

Sesame Ramen Salad

Serves 1

Prep time: 10 minutes • **Cook time:** 2 minutes • **Total time:** 12 minutes

▣ Microwave

15 Minutes, Cheap Eat, Vegetarian

Ramen is a college kitchen pantry essential. The quick-cooking curly noodles are the perfect base for this vegetable-rich salad. Served warm or cold, this salad makes a great quick lunch between classes. You can even pack it up and take it with you for lunch on the go.

1 package ramen, seasoning packet discarded

½ cup water

1 avocado, sliced

1 scallion, chopped

¼ cup edamame

¼ cup shredded carrots

2 tablespoons slivered almonds

2 tablespoons sesame ginger salad dressing

1. Break up the ramen and put them into a medium microwave-safe bowl.

2. Add the water to the noodles and microwave on HIGH (100% power) for 1 minute.

3. Continue to microwave in 30-second increments until the noodles are tender. Drain the noodles and put them back into the same bowl.

4. Add the avocado, scallion, edamame, carrots, and almonds to the ramen. Toss to combine.

5. Drizzle the salad dressing over the top and toss to combine.

Appliance Switch-Up: To cook the ramen on a stove or hot plate, bring 2½ cups of water to a boil in a medium saucepan. Carefully add the dried ramen to the boiling water. Using a spoon, push the noodles down to keep them fully submerged in the boiling water. Boil for 2 minutes, drain the noodles, and put them in a medium bowl. Then continue with steps 4 and 5 as directed.

Nutty Broccoli Salad

Serves 1

Prep time: 10 minutes • **Total time:** 10 minutes

No Cook

15 Minutes, Healthy, Vegetarian

Broccoli is a nutritional powerhouse and it's very filling. This crunchy salad is sure to keep you full and satisfied during a long day of classes. Make a double batch, because this salad keeps well in the refrigerator for up to 4 days. Enjoy this salad on its own or with Lemony Cod (page 98).

2 cups small broccoli florets

2 tablespoons diced red onion

2 tablespoons dried cranberries

2 tablespoons pepitas

2 tablespoons almonds, chopped

2 tablespoons honey mustard salad dressing

1. Put the broccoli florets into a medium bowl.

2. Add the onion, cranberries, pepitas, and almonds. Toss to combine.

3. Drizzle the salad dressing over the top and toss to combine.

Smart Shopping: Many grocery stores offer bulk bins where you can buy nuts, seeds, and other grains by weight instead of in individual packages. Buying the almonds and pepitas for this recipe from the bulk bins is a great way to save money because you can purchase the exact amount you need to make the recipe.

Tuna Salad Avocado Bowls

Makes 2 avocado bowls

Prep time: 5 minutes • **Total time:** 5 minutes

No Cook

15 Minutes, 5 or Fewer Ingredients, Cheap Eat, Healthy

I love these Tuna Salad Avocado Bowls, because you eat them right out of the avocado shell, which means fewer dishes to clean up. Or, if you prefer, you can spoon the salad onto your favorite bread and enjoy it as a sandwich.

1 (5-ounce) can albacore tuna, drained

1 ripe avocado

2 tablespoons diced red onion

1 tablespoon mayonnaise

1 tablespoon lime juice

⅛ teaspoon salt

Pinch ground black pepper

1. Put the drained tuna in a medium bowl.

2. Cut the avocado in half, remove the pit, and scoop most of the avocado flesh from the skin, leaving a thin layer in the skin. Reserve the avocado skins.

3. Put the avocado flesh into the mixing bowl with the tuna. Using a fork, mash the avocado and tuna together.

4. Add the onion, mayonnaise, lime juice, salt, and pepper to the tuna mixture and stir to combine.

5. Spoon half of the tuna mixture into each of the reserved avocado halves.

Recipe Remix: This recipe is great using any type of canned protein. You can use the same amount of canned chicken or crab in place of the tuna.

Veggie Gyros

Makes 1 gyro

Prep time: 5 minutes • **Cook time:** 10 seconds • **Total time:** 5 minutes

▢ Microwave

15 Minutes, Cheap Eat, Healthy, Vegetarian

This gyro is jam-packed with fresh veggies and protein-rich chickpeas. You can roll this up as a gyro, as directed, or cut the pita in half and add half of each ingredient into the pocket of each half pita. The tzatziki is a creamy yogurt-based sauce made with cucumber, herbs, and lemon juice. It's great on this gyro, but you can also use it as a dip for veggie or pita chips.

1 pita

½ cup romaine lettuce, chopped

½ tomato, diced

¼ cup cucumber, peeled and diced

2 tablespoons canned chickpeas (garbanzo beans), drained

2 tablespoons red onion, diced

2 tablespoons tzatziki

1 tablespoon crumbled feta cheese, divided

1. Wrap the pita in a damp paper towel and microwave on HIGH (100% power) for 10 seconds.

2. Put the lettuce, tomato, cucumber, chickpeas, and onion on top of the pita.

3. Drizzle with tzatziki and top with feta cheese.

4. Roll the pita up to eat.

Make It Yourself: To make your own tzatziki, grate ½ of a peeled cucumber. Wrap the grated cucumber in a paper towel and squeeze it to remove the excess water. Put the grated cucumber into a medium bowl and combine with ¾ cup plain Greek yogurt, 1 tablespoon olive oil, ½ tablespoon lemon juice, ½ tablespoon red wine vinegar, ½ tablespoon chopped fresh dill, 1 minced garlic clove, and 1 teaspoon salt. Stir until fully combined.

Lemon Pepper Tuna Lettuce Wraps

Makes 3 lettuce wraps

Prep time: 5 minutes • **Total time:** 5 minutes

No Cook

15 Minutes, Cheap Eat, Healthy

These delicious wraps are a low-carb, yet satisfying, meal. My favorite part of this recipe is the garlic aioli. This garlicky mayonnaise sauce adds incredible flavor to these wraps. You can also use it as a condiment for The Perfect Burger (page 95).

1 (5-ounce) can albacore tuna, drained

2 teaspoons lemon pepper seasoning

3 Boston Bibb or butter lettuce leaves

½ avocado, sliced

½ tomato, sliced

¼ cup mayonnaise

1 garlic clove, minced

1 teaspoon lemon juice

¼ teaspoon salt

1. Put the tuna into a medium bowl.

2. Add the lemon pepper seasoning and use a fork to combine, breaking up the tuna as you stir.

3. Lay out the lettuce leaves on a plate.

4. Layer 2 to 3 avocado slices and 1 to 2 tomato slices on each lettuce leaf. Then, put one-third of the tuna on top of the avocado and tomato in each wrap.

5. In a small bowl, make the garlic aioli by mixing together the mayonnaise, garlic, lemon juice, and salt.

6. Drizzle the mayonnaise mixture on top of the tuna in each wrap.

7. Fold the lettuce leaves like a taco to eat.

Recipe Remix: You can easily turn these wraps into a salad. Chop the lettuce or use leftover lettuce from another meal. Put the chopped lettuce into a bowl and top with chopped avocado, tomato, and the seasoned tuna. Drizzle garlic aioli over the top.

Turkey Club Wraps

Makes 1 wrap

Prep time: 5 minutes • **Total time:** 5 minutes

No Cook

15 Minutes, Cheap Eat

A Turkey Club is a classic sandwich with layers of turkey, bacon, and cheese, usually served on toast. In this recipe, a spinach tortilla wrap replaces the toast, turning the sandwich into an easy portable meal. Wrap it up and eat it on your way to class.

1 tablespoon mayonnaise

1 spinach tortilla wrap

1 teaspoon brown mustard

2 slices deli turkey

2 slices deli cheddar cheese

2 slices Microwave Bacon (page 44)

4 slices avocado

2 slices tomato

1 cup shredded iceberg lettuce

1. Spread the mayonnaise over one side of the tortilla, leaving a 1-inch border around the edge.

2. Spread the brown mustard on top of the mayonnaise.

3. Layer the turkey, cheddar cheese, bacon, avocado, tomato, and lettuce on top of the mustard.

4. Fold the sides of the tortilla in about 2 inches. Then, starting at one end, roll the tortilla up.

Recipe Remix: Turn this turkey wrap into a Buffalo chicken wrap by swapping out the mayonnaise for blue cheese salad dressing, the mustard for the same amount of hot sauce, the turkey for the same amount of deli Buffalo chicken, and the avocado for ¼ cup chopped celery. Serve it with or without the bacon.

Chicken Caesar Wraps

Makes 1 wrap

Prep time: 5 minutes • **Total time:** 5 minutes

No Cook

15 Minutes, Cheap Eat, Healthy

My family is obsessed with Caesar salad, so I'm always coming up with new ways to serve it. These Chicken Caesar Wraps are one of our favorite combinations. You can use any type of cooked chicken in these wraps, such as deli chicken, canned chicken, rotisserie chicken, or leftover chicken. The chopped, flavored croutons add an unexpected crunch.

½ cup cooked, shredded chicken

¾ cup chopped romaine lettuce

¼ cup halved cherry tomatoes

2 tablespoons grated Parmesan cheese

2 tablespoons Caesar-flavored croutons, chopped

3 tablespoons Caesar salad dressing

1 whole wheat tortilla wrap

1. In a medium bowl, combine the chicken, lettuce, tomatoes, Parmesan cheese, croutons, and salad dressing. Toss to combine.

2. Spread the mixture over the tortilla, leaving a 1-inch border around the edge.

3. Fold the sides of the tortilla in about 2 inches. Then, starting at one end, roll the tortilla up.

Make It Yourself: To make your own Caesar salad dressing, put ½ cup mayonnaise, ¼ cup grated Parmesan cheese, 1 chopped garlic clove, 1 tablespoon lemon juice, ½ teaspoon anchovy paste, ½ teaspoon Dijon mustard, ½ teaspoon Worcestershire sauce, ⅛ teaspoon salt, and ⅛ teaspoon ground black pepper into a blender and blend until smooth.

Cobb Salad Pitas

Serves 1

Prep time: 5 minutes • **Cook time:** 10 seconds • **Total time:** 5 minutes

Microwave

15 Minutes

These wraps have all of the classic Cobb salad toppings stuffed into a soft pita. This makes a great sandwich, or you can pile all of the ingredients into a salad bowl, toss them together, and serve with pita wedges on the side. You can also serve this as a gyro. In step 2, do not cut the pita in half. Instead, pile all of the ingredients on top of the whole pita and roll it up.

1 pita

1 cup chopped lettuce

½ **avocado, diced**

½ **tomato, diced**

1 **hard-boiled egg, diced**

2 **slices deli chicken, chopped**

2 **slices deli ham, chopped**

4 **slices Microwave Bacon (page 44), chopped**

¼ **cup shredded cheddar cheese**

¼ **cup avocado ranch salad dressing**

1. Wrap the pita in a damp paper towel and microwave on HIGH (100% power) for 10 seconds.

2. Cut the pita in half and put ½ cup of the lettuce, half of the avocado, half of the tomato, half of the egg, half of the chicken, half of the ham, half of the bacon, and 2 tablespoons of the cheddar cheese into each half of the pita.

3. Drizzle 2 tablespoons of salad dressing over each half.

Smart Shopping: Usually, deli items are ordered by weight. However, you can ask the deli clerk to give you a specific number of slices of deli meat or cheese. This is a great way to get the exact amount you need to make the recipe.

Caprese Chicken Grilled Cheese Sandwiches

Makes 1 sandwich

Prep time: 5 minutes • **Cook time:** 6 minutes • **Total time:** 11 minutes

Hot Plate/Stove

15 Minutes

This grilled cheese is great using regular sandwich bread or a heartier bread like ciabatta or sourdough. It's a great way to use up leftover pesto and shredded mozzarella from Spinach Pesto Flatbread Pizzas (page 84).

1 tablespoon
    store-bought pesto

2 slices sandwich bread

2 slices deli chicken

3 slices tomato

½ cup shredded
    mozzarella cheese

1 tablespoon unsalted
    butter, divided

1. Preheat a skillet over medium heat.

2. Brush ½ tablespoon of the pesto on one side of each slice of bread.

3. On top of the pesto, pile the chicken on one piece of bread.

4. Top the chicken with the tomato slices and mozzarella cheese.

5. Top with the remaining slice of bread, pesto-side down.

6. Spread ½ tablespoon of the butter on top of the sandwich.

7. When the skillet is hot, carefully place the sandwich, butter-side down, into the skillet.

8. Spread the remaining ½ tablespoon of butter on the top of the sandwich.

9. Cook for about 3 minutes, or until the bottom of the sandwich is toasted and golden.

10. Using a spatula, carefully flip the sandwich and toast for another 3 minutes, or until the bottom is toasted and golden and the cheese has melted.

Appliance Switch-Up: To make this in a toaster oven, preheat the baking sheet in the toaster oven at 425°F. Prepare the sandwich as directed. Using oven mitts, place the sandwich on the preheated baking sheet and bake for 3 to 4 minutes, or until the bottom of the sandwich is toasted and golden. Flip the sandwich and bake for another 3 to 4 minutes or until the other side of the sandwich is toasted and the cheese has melted.

Ultimate Roast Beef Sandwiches

Makes 1 sandwich

Prep time: 5 minutes • **Total time:** 5 minutes

No Cook

15 Minutes

This sandwich has layer upon layer of amazing flavors. The buttery brioche bun, zippy horseradish sauce, and fresh arugula pack a nice punch. My favorite part is the French-fried onions that add an unmistakable crunch and even more flavor. You can usually find the French-fried onions in the condiment aisle of the grocery store.

2 tablespoons creamy horseradish sauce

1 brioche bun

2 thin slices deli cheddar cheese

4 thin slices deli roast beef

2 tablespoons French-fried onions

½ cup baby arugula

1. Spread the horseradish sauce on the insides of the brioche bun.

2. Lay the cheddar cheese slices on the bottom half of the bun.

3. Pile the roast beef, onions, and arugula on top of the cheese.

4. Cover with the top of the bun.

Make It Yourself: If you can't find bottled horseradish sauce, make it yourself. In a small bowl, mix together ¼ cup sour cream, 1 tablespoon drained prepared horseradish, 1 tablespoon mayonnaise, ½ teaspoon apple cider vinegar, ⅛ teaspoon salt, and a pinch of ground black pepper.

Buffalo Chicken Flatbreads

Makes 1 flatbread

Prep time: 5 minutes • **Cook time:** 1 minute • **Total time:** 6 minutes

▢ Microwave

15 Minutes

This recipe has all of the flavors of hot wings piled onto a tender flatbread. Using store-bought packaged coleslaw is a great hack. Go for the traditional coleslaw mixes, such as cabbage and carrots, or use a broccoli slaw mixture for added nutrition.

1 cup cooked, shredded chicken

¼ cup hot sauce

1 tablespoon unsalted butter

1 flatbread or naan

1 cup packaged coleslaw

½ cup finely diced celery

¼ cup blue cheese salad dressing

1. Put the chicken, hot sauce, and butter into a medium microwave-safe bowl. Microwave on HIGH (100% power) for 1 minute, or until the chicken is warmed through.

2. Stir the chicken mixture and spread it on top of the flatbread.

3. In a medium bowl, combine the coleslaw, celery, and salad dressing.

4. Spoon the coleslaw on top of the chicken.

Appliance Switch-Up: To make the chicken mixture on a stovetop or hot plate, put the chicken, hot sauce, and butter into a small saucepan and cook over medium-high heat for 3 to 4 minutes or until the chicken is warmed through.

Vegetarian Chili, page 87

CHAPTER 6

SOLO MEALS

Spinach Pesto Flatbread Pizzas 84

Bean and Cheese Quesadillas 85

Vegetarian Burrito Bowls 86

Vegetarian Chili 87

Veggie Ramen 88

Microwave Risotto 89

Loaded Baked Potatoes 90

Microwave Mac & Cheese 91

Microwave Chicken Enchiladas 92

Microwave Parmesan Chicken 93

Baked Chicken Tenders 94

The Perfect Burger 95

Italian Pork Chops 96

Lemony Cod 98

Southwest Black Bean Soup 99

Spinach Pesto Flatbread Pizzas

Serves 1

Prep time: 5 minutes • **Cook time:** 10 minutes • **Total time:** 15 minutes

⌨ Oven

15 Minutes, 5 or Fewer Ingredients, Cheap Eat, Healthy, Vegetarian

These flatbread pizzas use store-bought naan as the crust. Naan is a traditional Indian flatbread that is tender and chewy, making it the perfect base for pizza. You can use pre-shredded low-moisture mozzarella for this recipe. But, if you want to treat yourself, slice up fresh, whole-milk mozzarella into ⅛-inch slices to top your pizza.

¼ cup store-bought pesto, divided

2 naan flatbreads

½ cup shredded mozzarella, divided

¼ cup baby spinach, divided

¼ teaspoon salt

Pinch ground black pepper

1. Preheat the oven to 425°F.

2. Line a rimmed baking sheet with parchment paper or aluminum foil and set aside.

3. Spread 2 tablespoons of pesto evenly on the first naan, then top with ¼ cup of the mozzarella and 2 tablespoons of the baby spinach.

4. Season each naan with ⅛ teaspoon of salt and a pinch of pepper. Repeat with the remaining naan.

5. Bake for 8 to 10 minutes or until the cheese has melted.

Make It Yourself: To make pesto from scratch, put 1 cup fresh basil leaves, 2 tablespoons pine nuts, 2 garlic cloves, and ¼ cup Parmesan cheese into a blender and blend until finely chopped. With the blender running, pour in ¼ cup olive oil until the mixture emulsifies. Season with ⅛ teaspoon salt and a pinch of ground black pepper.

Bean and Cheese Quesadillas

Serves 1

Prep time: 5 minutes • **Cook time:** 4 minutes • **Total time:** 9 minutes

Hot Plate/Stove

15 Minutes, 5 or Fewer Ingredients, Cheap Eat, Healthy, Vegetarian

These quesadillas make a hearty, meatless meal. This recipe is a great way to use up leftover black beans from Southwest Black Bean Soup (page 99) or shredded cheese and tortillas from Microwave Chicken Enchiladas (page 92).

1 (8-inch) whole-grain flour tortilla

½ cup shredded cheddar cheese, divided

¼ cup canned black beans, drained

1 tablespoon chopped red onion or scallion

1 teaspoon butter, divided

1. Heat a medium skillet over medium heat.

2. Meanwhile, place the tortilla on a cutting board or work surface. Sprinkle ¼ cup of the cheddar cheese on half of the tortilla.

3. Top with the black beans, onion, and the remaining ¼ cup of cheese.

4. Fold the tortilla in half. Spread ½ teaspoon of the butter on the top of the quesadilla.

5. Carefully, flip the quesadilla into the preheated skillet, butter-side down.

6. Spread the remaining ½ teaspoon of butter on the top of the quesadilla.

7. Cook the quesadilla for 2 minutes.

8. Carefully, flip the quesadilla and cook for 1 to 2 minutes longer, or until the bottom is golden and crispy.

Appliance Switch-Up: To make this in a toaster oven, place a baking sheet in the toaster oven and preheat it to 425°F. Prepare as directed. Using oven mitts, place the quesadilla on the preheated baking sheet. Bake for 2 to 3 minutes on each side, or until the cheese has melted.

Vegetarian Burrito Bowls

Serves 1

Prep time: 5 minutes • **Cook time:** 2 minutes • **Total time:** 7 minutes

Microwave

15 Minutes, Healthy, Vegetarian

These burrito bowls are one of my go-to quick dinners. I love using jasmine rice, but whole-grain brown rice is another healthier option. You can easily change up the toppings to use what you have on hand. Try adding your favorite protein, like cooked chicken, beef, or pork.

1 cup cooked rice

1 cup chopped lettuce

¼ cup salsa

¼ cup canned corn, drained

¼ cup canned black beans, drained

¼ cup chopped tomato

¼ cup chopped avocado

1 lime, halved

3 tablespoons chipotle ranch salad dressing

1. Put the cooked rice into a serving bowl.

2. Top it with the lettuce, salsa, corn, black beans, tomato, and avocado.

3. Squeeze the lime juice over the burrito bowl.

4. Drizzle the salad dressing over the top.

Make It Yourself: To make your own chipotle ranch dressing, in a small bowl, whisk together ½ cup sour cream, ½ teaspoon chipotle pepper sauce, 1 minced garlic clove, ⅛ teaspoon salt, and the juice from half of a lime.

Vegetarian Chili

Serves 1

Prep time: 5 minutes • **Cook time:** 6 minutes 30 seconds • **Total time:** 12 minutes

Microwave

15 Minutes, Cheap Eat, Healthy, Vegetarian

This hearty chili tastes like it was simmered all day, but it comes together in less than 15 minutes! I like to top mine with shredded Monterey Jack cheese, a dollop of sour cream, and a sprinkling of chopped scallions.

¼ cup diced bell pepper

2 tablespoons diced onion

1 garlic clove, minced

1 tablespoon unsalted butter

½ teaspoon ground cumin

½ teaspoon paprika

Pinch chili powder

1 (15-ounce) can diced tomatoes, drained and juice reserved

¼ cup canned kidney beans, drained

½ teaspoon salt

1. In a medium microwave-safe bowl, combine the bell pepper, onion, garlic, butter, cumin, paprika, and chili powder.

2. Microwave on HIGH (100% power) for 30 seconds, then stir.

3. Stir in the tomatoes, kidney beans, and salt.

4. Cover the bowl with plastic wrap and make three 1-inch slits in it.

5. Microwave on HIGH for 2 minutes. Stir, then let stand for 1 minute.

6. If the chili is too dry, add some of the reserved tomato juice until it reaches your desired consistency.

7. Replace the plastic wrap and microwave on MEDIUM (50% power) for 2 minutes. Stir, then let stand for 1 minute before serving.

Make It Even Faster: Dicing peppers and onions can be time consuming. Save time by using frozen chopped onions and peppers. You can thaw them or, if using frozen, add an additional 1 minute of cook time in step 7.

Veggie Ramen

Serves 1

Prep time: 5 minutes • **Cook time:** 3 minutes • **Total time:** 8 minutes

▢ Microwave

15 Minutes, Cheap Eat, Vegetarian

What could be more affordable and easier to make than ramen? This vegetarian recipe takes plain ramen to the next level by adding mixed vegetables and a flavorful broth. I also like to add a soft-boiled egg and a drizzle of hot chili garlic sauce.

1 (3-ounce) package ramen, seasoning packet discarded

2 cups vegetable broth

1 garlic clove, minced

¼ cup frozen mixed vegetables

¼ cup sliced mushrooms

1 tablespoon sliced scallion

1. In a large microwave-safe bowl, combine the ramen, broth, garlic, mixed vegetables, and mushrooms.

2. Microwave on HIGH (100% power) for 2 to 3 minutes, or until the noodles are tender and the vegetables are warmed through.

3. Top the ramen with the scallion.

Recipe Remix: For more protein, add ½ cup leftover cooked chicken, pork, or beef to the bowl in step 1.

Microwave Risotto

Serves 1

Prep time: 5 minutes • **Cook time:** 22 minutes • **Total time:** 27 minutes

Microwave

Cheap Eat, Vegetarian

Risotto is a decadent rice dish made with arborio rice—a type of short-grain rice that has a high starch content. This easy microwave version has all the flavors and texture of the stovetop version without the fuss.

1½ tablespoons unsalted butter

1 garlic clove, minced

¼ cup onion, minced

¾ cups vegetable broth

1 cup arborio rice

⅓ cup white wine, or additional vegetable broth

2 tablespoons grated Parmesan cheese

1. In a large microwave-safe bowl, combine the butter, garlic, and onion. Microwave on HIGH (100% power) for 3 minutes. Remove the bowl from the microwave and set aside.

2. Pour the vegetable broth into a medium microwave-safe bowl. Microwave on HIGH for 2 to 3 minutes, or until hot but not boiling.

3. Put the hot broth and arborio rice into the bowl with the onion mixture.

4. Cover the bowl with plastic wrap and microwave on HIGH for 6 minutes.

5. Carefully, remove the bowl and uncover it (it will be very hot). Discard the plastic wrap.

6. Stir in the white wine and microwave on HIGH for 10 minutes.

7. Carefully, remove the bowl from the microwave and stir in the Parmesan cheese.

Recipe Remix: During the last 2 minutes of cooking in step 6, stir in ¼ cup frozen peas, ½ cup chopped asparagus or ½ cup cooked chicken. You could also stir in 1 tablespoon pesto or 2 tablespoons jarred marinara sauce during step 7.

Loaded Baked Potatoes

Serves 1

Prep time: 5 minutes • **Cook time:** 8 minutes • **Total time:** 13 minutes

☐ Microwave

15 Minutes, Cheap Eat

This baked potato is a meal in itself. You can pile it high with the toppings listed below or replace the bacon with a hearty portion of Vegetarian Chili (page 87).

1 russet potato

1 teaspoon olive oil

¼ teaspoon salt, divided

Ground black pepper

1 tablespoon unsalted butter

2 tablespoons shredded cheddar cheese

1 tablespoon sour cream

1 slice Microwave Bacon (page 44), crumbled

1 tablespoon chopped scallion

1. Using a fork, pierce the potato skin 3 to 4 times on all sides. Using a paper towel, rub the olive oil all over the potato skin. Season the outside of the potato with ⅛ teaspoon salt and a pinch of pepper.

2. Place the potato on a microwave-safe plate and microwave on HIGH (100% power) for 5 minutes. Flip the potato and microwave on HIGH for another 3 minutes.

3. The potato is done cooking when you can pierce it with a fork easily. If you feel some resistance, continue to microwave on HIGH in 1-minute increments until the potato is fork tender.

4. Carefully remove the potato from the microwave and cut it lengthwise, without cutting all the way through.

5. Season the potato with the remaining ⅛ teaspoon of salt and pepper. Top with the butter, cheddar cheese, sour cream, bacon, and scallion.

Appliance Switch-Up: To make these in the oven, preheat to 450°F. After piercing the potato, place it on a baking sheet and bake for 25 minutes. Remove the potato from the oven, coat it in oil, and season with salt and pepper. Return to the oven and bake for 20 minutes more. Follow steps 3 through 5.

Microwave Mac & Cheese

Serves 1

Prep time: 5 minutes • **Cook time:** 7 minutes • **Total time:** 12 minutes

▢ **Microwave**

15 Minutes, 5 or Fewer Ingredients, Cheap Eat, Vegetarian

This classic comfort food is the perfect lunch, dinner, or late-night snack. Best of all, it can be ready in under 15 minutes with only a few ingredients. To make this Microwave Mac & Cheese even faster, use pre-shredded cheese. If you have leftover cheese, you can freeze it for another time.

⅓ **cup whole-grain elbow pasta**

½ **cup plus 2 tablespoons water**

Pinch salt

⅓ **cup shredded cheddar Jack cheese**

2 teaspoons milk

Pinch ground black pepper

1. In a medium microwave-safe bowl, combine the pasta, water, and salt.

2. Microwave on HIGH (100% power) for 6 minutes, stirring after each 2-minute interval. Make sure that the water doesn't dry up. If it does, add water 1 tablespoon at a time.

3. After 6 minutes, there should be a small amount of thick water at the bottom of the bowl.

4. Stir in the cheddar Jack cheese and microwave on HIGH for another 20 to 30 seconds, or until the cheese has melted.

5. Add the milk and pepper and stir until everything is combined.

Make It Yourself: To add a crispy topping, mix together 2 tablespoons panko bread crumbs with ½ tablespoon melted butter and sprinkle it on top after step 5. Microwave on HIGH for 30 to 45 seconds.

Microwave Chicken Enchiladas

Serves 1

Prep time: 5 minutes • **Cook time:** 5 minutes • **Total time:** 10 minutes

🔲 Microwave

15 Minutes, 5 or Fewer Ingredients, Cheap Eat

My family loves enchiladas. I created this easy microwave version so my son could make one anytime he has a craving. Plan ahead for this recipe and make extra Microwave Parmesan Chicken (page 93) to use in this recipe.

¼ cup enchilada sauce, divided

¼ cup cooked, shredded chicken

¼ cup Mexican or taco blend shredded cheese, divided

1 (8-inch) corn or flour tortilla

Sour cream, salsa, and hot sauce, for topping (optional)

1. Spread 2 tablespoons of enchilada sauce over the bottom of a 9-by-9-inch microwave-safe baking dish.

2. In a small bowl, combine the chicken and 3 tablespoons of the cheese.

3. Place the tortilla on a dinner plate and spread the remaining 2 tablespoons of enchilada sauce all over both sides of the tortilla.

4. Spoon the chicken and cheese mixture near the edge of the tortilla in a straight line.

5. Tightly roll the tortilla up and place it on the baking dish with the enchilada sauce.

6. Top the rolled-up tortilla with the remaining tablespoon of cheese.

7. Wrap the baking dish loosely with plastic wrap and microwave on HIGH (100% power) for 5 minutes or until the cheese has melted.

8. Serve with desired toppings.

Recipe Remix: For a meatless enchilada, replace the chicken with the same amount of canned black beans. Drain the beans and mash them before adding them in step 2.

Microwave Parmesan Chicken

Serves 1

Prep time: 5 minutes • **Cook time:** 5 minutes • **Total time:** 10 minutes

▢ Microwave

15 Minutes, 5 or Fewer Ingredients, Healthy

After a long day in class, you can whip up this easy microwave chicken in under 15 minutes. Make extra so you can use the leftovers in other recipes like Caprese Chicken Grilled Cheese Sandwiches (page 78) or Buffalo Chicken Flatbreads (page 81).

1 (4-ounce) boneless, skinless chicken breast

2 teaspoons reduced-sodium soy sauce

⅛ teaspoon garlic powder

Pinch ground black pepper

2 tablespoons grated Parmesan cheese

½ teaspoon unsalted butter

1. Place the chicken in a 9-by-9-inch microwave-safe baking dish.

2. Drizzle the soy sauce over the chicken.

3. Sprinkle the garlic powder, pepper, and Parmesan cheese over the chicken.

4. Place the butter in dollops on top of the chicken.

5. Cover the baking dish with plastic wrap and microwave on HIGH (100% power) for 4 to 5 minutes, or until the internal temperature of the chicken reaches 165°F.

Make It Even Faster: To speed up the cooking time, cut the chicken horizontally into two ¼-inch-thick pieces. Place the cutlets side by side, but not touching, in the baking dish and microwave on HIGH for 3 to 4 minutes, or until the internal temperature of the chicken reaches 165°F.

Baked Chicken Tenders

Serves 1

Prep time: 5 minutes • **Cook time:** 22 minutes • **Total time:** 27 minutes

Oven

Cheap Eat, Healthy

These chicken tenders are a healthy and delicious alternative to the deep-fried version. You can easily change up this basic recipe by swapping the garlic powder, onion powder, and paprika for ½ teaspoon taco seasoning.

1 tablespoon unsalted butter

½ teaspoon salt

¼ teaspoon ground black pepper

¼ teaspoon paprika

⅛ teaspoon garlic powder

⅛ teaspoon onion powder

4 ounces boneless, skinless chicken breast tenders

¼ cup flour

1. Preheat the oven to 400°F.

2. Put the butter on a rimmed baking sheet, then put the baking sheet in the preheated oven until the butter has melted.

3. In a small bowl, combine the salt, pepper, paprika, garlic powder, and onion powder and stir.

4. Lay the chicken on a cutting board and season with half of the salt mixture.

5. Put the flour and the remaining half of the seasoning mixture into a zip-top bag.

6. Put the chicken tenders into the bag with the flour mixture. Seal the bag and shake until the chicken is fully coated.

7. Arrange the chicken on the baking sheet without letting them touch. Bake for 10 minutes.

8. Flip the chicken and bake for another 10 to 12 minutes, or until the internal temperature of the chicken reaches 165°F.

Smart Shopping: Make your own chicken tenders by slicing a boneless, skinless chicken breast horizontally into two thinner pieces and then slice each piece into ½-inch-thick strips.

The Perfect Burger

Serves 1

Prep time: 5 minutes • **Cook time:** 10 minutes • **Total time:** 15 minutes

Hot Plate/Stove

15 Minutes, Cheap Eat

The key to a juicy burger is to use an 80/20 blend of meat—80 percent lean to 20 percent fat. Pair with Everything Bagel Potato Chips (page 48) to make it a meal.

⅓ **pound ground chuck**

¼ **teaspoon Worcestershire sauce**

⅛ **teaspoon salt**

⅛ **teaspoon garlic powder**

⅛ **teaspoon onion powder**

⅛ **teaspoon ground black pepper**

1 **teaspoon canola oil**

Cheese, lettuce tomato, and onion, for topping (optional)

1 **hamburger bun**

1. In a medium bowl, combine the ground chuck, Worcestershire sauce, salt, garlic powder, onion powder, and pepper.

2. Using your hands, gently mix until just combined. Be careful not to overmix.

3. Shape the meat into a ¾-inch-thick patty. Then, use your thumb to make an indentation in the center of the patty to keep the burger from puffing up as it cooks.

4. In a small skillet, heat the canola oil over high heat.

5. When the oil is hot, carefully place the burger patty in the skillet and cook for 5 minutes.

6. Flip the burger patty and cook it on the other side for 5 minutes (for medium-well), or until the internal temperature of the burger reaches 160°F.

7. If you want to add cheese, turn off the heat, place a slice of your favorite cheese on top of the patty, and cover the skillet with aluminum foil. Allow the burger patty to sit for 1 to 2 minutes, or until the cheese has melted. Serve on the hamburger bun.

Recipe Remix: Swap out ground beef for ground turkey. Prepare and cook the turkey burger the same as a ground beef burger until the internal temperature reaches 165°F.

Italian Pork Chops

Serves 1

Prep time: 5 minutes • **Cook time:** 14 minutes • **Total time:** 19 minutes

Hot Plate/Stove

Cheap Eat, Healthy

These juicy pork chops with a buttery lemon sauce are sure to impress your friends. The key to not overcooking your meat is to use a meat thermometer to know exactly when it's done. It's hard to tell when meat is cooked through just by looking at it.

½ **teaspoon salt**

¼ **teaspoon ground black pepper**

¼ **teaspoon garlic powder**

¼ **teaspoon onion powder**

1 **(6-ounce) boneless pork chop**

1 **tablespoon Italian seasoning**

2 **teaspoons olive oil**

1 **garlic clove, sliced thin**

1 **tablespoon unsalted butter**

¼ **cup chicken broth**

Juice of ½ **lemon**

1. In a small bowl, combine the salt, pepper, garlic powder, and onion powder.

2. Season both sides of the pork chop with the salt mixture.

3. Using your hands, coat both sides of the pork chop evenly with the Italian seasoning, pressing it into the pork chop. Set aside.

4. In a small skillet, heat the oil over medium-high heat. Add the garlic and cook for 30 seconds, or until fragrant, stirring it constantly so it doesn't burn.

5. Put the pork chop in the skillet and cook for 3 to 4 minutes. Flip and cook for 3 to 4 minutes more, or until the internal temperature of the pork reaches 145°F.

6. Transfer the pork chop to a plate and cover it with foil.

7. To make the sauce, put the butter into the same skillet and let it melt.

8. Whisk in the broth and lemon juice, and simmer for 3 minutes, or until the sauce is reduced by half.

9. Drizzle the sauce over the pork chop.

Make It Even Faster: To speed up this recipe, slice a 6-ounce pork chop in half horizontally into two ½-inch-thick pieces, and reduce the cooking time to 2 to 3 minutes per side or until a meat thermometer reaches 145°F.

Lemony Cod

Serves 1

Prep time: 5 minutes • **Cook time:** 6 minutes • **Total time:** 11 minutes

▢ Microwave

15 Minutes, Healthy

This light and healthy meal is quick and easy to make. You can enjoy this cod on its own or use it to make a fish taco. Top your fish taco with a handful of packaged coleslaw, chopped avocado, and chipotle ranch salad dressing.

¼ cup chopped tomato

1 tablespoon finely diced onion

1½ teaspoons water

1 teaspoon lemon juice

½ teaspoon canola oil

½ teaspoon minced garlic

¼ teaspoon dried parsley

⅛ teaspoon dried basil

⅛ teaspoon salt

Pinch paprika

Pinch ground black pepper

1 (4-ounce) cod fillet

1. In a small bowl, combine the tomato, onion, water, lemon juice, canola oil, garlic, dried parsley, dried basil, salt, paprika, and pepper.

2. Place the cod fillet in a 9-by-9-inch microwave-safe baking dish.

3. Top the cod with the tomato mixture and cover the dish with plastic wrap.

4. Microwave on HIGH (100% power) for 5 to 6 minutes or until the internal temperature of the cod reaches 145°F.

Make It Even Faster: Skip peeling and mincing fresh garlic by using jarred minced garlic. It's fast and easy and won't leave you with messy hands.

Southwest Black Bean Soup

Serves 1

Prep time: 5 minutes • **Cook time:** 3 minutes • **Total time:** 8 minutes

Microwave

15 Minutes, Cheap Eat, Healthy, Vegetarian

This meatless soup is one of my favorite fast meals. It's ready in less than 10 minutes, so it's perfect for a quick lunch or satisfying dinner. For a heartier version, serve it with Bean and Cheese Quesadillas (page 85).

½ cup canned black beans, drained

½ cup vegetable broth

¼ cup salsa

¼ cup whole kernel corn

⅛ teaspoon taco seasoning

⅛ teaspoon salt

¼ cup shredded cheddar cheese

2 teaspoons chopped scallion

Lime wedge

1. In a large microwave-safe bowl, combine the black beans, vegetable broth, salsa, corn, taco seasoning, and salt. Mix well.

2. Microwave on HIGH (100% power) for 2 to 3 minutes, or until the soup is hot all the way through.

3. Carefully, remove the soup from the microwave and top it with the cheddar cheese, scallion, and a squeeze of lime juice.

Appliance Switch-Up: To make this recipe on a stove or hot plate, in a small saucepan, combine the beans, broth, salsa, corn, taco seasoning, and salt. Simmer over medium-high heat for 5 minutes, then transfer to a serving bowl and add toppings as directed in step 3.

Microwave BBQ Chicken Nachos, page 114

CHAPTER 7

FEAST WITH FRIENDS

Zesty Spaghetti Squash Salad 102

Microwave Spaghetti Marinara 104

Creamy Fettuccine Alfredo 105

Ravioli Lasagna 106

Crispy Oven "Fried" Chicken 108

Baked Ham and Cheese Sliders 110

Brown Sugar Garlic Pork Medallions 112

Microwave BBQ Chicken Nachos 114

Microwave Meat Loaf 115

Miso-Glazed Salmon 116

Zesty Spaghetti Squash Salad

Serves 6

Prep time: 10 minutes • **Cook time:** 10 minutes • **Total time:** 20 minutes

Microwave

Healthy, Vegetarian

Spaghetti squash is an interesting vegetable because, when it's cooked, the flesh of the squash resembles spaghetti. It has a firm texture and is a great substitute for pasta. To speed up this recipe, I like to prep the vegetables while the squash is cooking.

1 spaghetti squash

2 Roma tomatoes, seeded and diced

2 cups broccoli florets

1 cucumber, diced

2 bell peppers, seeded and diced

1 large red onion, diced

2 (2.25-ounce) cans sliced black olives, drained

1 (16-ounce) bottle zesty Italian salad dressing

¼ cup grated Parmesan cheese

½ teaspoon salt

¼ teaspoon ground black pepper

1. Using a knife, score one side of the squash, ⅛-inch deep, from the stem to the bottom. Repeat on the other side.

2. Using the same knife, lightly pierce the squash 8 to 10 times all over.

3. Place the squash in a large microwave-safe baking dish and microwave on HIGH (100% power) for 5 minutes.

4. Carefully remove the baking dish from the microwave and place the squash on a cutting board. Using a chef's knife, follow the scoring lines you made in step 1 and cut through to the middle of the squash. Use your hands to pry the squash apart into two halves. Remove the seeds from the center of the squash with a spoon.

5. Place the squash halves back into the baking dish, flesh-side down. Fill the baking dish with 1 inch of water (just enough to create a moist environment so the squash will steam) and microwave on HIGH for 5 minutes.

6. After 5 minutes, poke the skin on the squash with a fork. If the fork easily slides into the squash, it's done. If there is resistance, microwave on HIGH in 2-minute increments, testing for doneness after each cycle.

7. Carefully remove the baking dish from the microwave and transfer the squash to a cutting board.

8. Using a fork, scrape the "spaghetti" strands from the inside of the squash. Put the strands into a large bowl.

9. Add the tomatoes, broccoli, cucumber, bell peppers, and onion to the bowl. Toss until the ingredients are combined.

10. Pour the salad dressing over the salad and add the Parmesan cheese, salt, and black pepper. Toss until the ingredients are combined.

Make It Even Faster: To save prep time, go to the grocery store salad bar for pre-chopped vegetables, such as the cucumber, broccoli, bell pepper, and tomatoes in this recipe. You can also add other vegetables that you like.

Microwave Spaghetti Marinara

Serves 6

Prep time: 5 minutes • **Cook time:** 23 minutes, plus 5 minutes to cool
Total time: 33 minutes

▢ Microwave

5 or Fewer Ingredients, Cheap Eat, Vegetarian

Spaghetti marinara is a dish that shows up on many dinner tables across the country every week. You can boost the flavor of this recipe by adding extra vegetables. Chop mushrooms, zucchini, or eggplant into small dice and add them during step 1. The best part about this recipe is that there's only one dish to wash.

1 (28-ounce) jar marinara sauce

2 cups water

8 ounces spaghetti, broken into thirds

½ teaspoon salt

¼ teaspoon ground black pepper

½ cup grated Parmesan cheese

1. In a large microwave-safe baking dish, combine the marinara sauce, water, spaghetti pieces, salt, and pepper.

2. Cover the baking dish with plastic wrap and peel back one corner to vent.

3. Microwave on HIGH (100% power) for 5 minutes.

4. Carefully remove the baking dish from the microwave and stir well. Cover the baking dish again and microwave on HIGH for an additional 8 to 10 minutes.

5. Carefully remove the baking dish from the microwave and sprinkle the Parmesan cheese over the top. Cover the baking dish and return to the microwave and cook on HIGH for 7 to 8 minutes more, or until the spaghetti is tender.

6. Carefully remove the baking dish from the microwave and allow it to cool for 5 minutes before serving.

Smart Shopping: Try using marinara sauce that is pre-flavored with basil, onion, garlic, sausage, or meat.

Creamy Fettuccine Alfredo

Serves 6

Prep time: 5 minutes • **Cook time:** 10 minutes • **Total time:** 15 minutes

Microwave

15 Minutes, 5 or Fewer Ingredients, Cheap Eat, Vegetarian

If you're tired of takeout and jarred sauces, you'll love this recipe. This Creamy Fettuccine Alfredo can be made from scratch in 15 minutes. Alfredo sauce is a rich, decadent Parmesan cream sauce that is flavored with garlic. Serve it over pasta or add some leftover Microwave Parmesan Chicken (page 93) for added protein.

1 pint heavy cream

½ cup butter

1 teaspoon minced garlic

1 teaspoon salt

¼ teaspoon ground black pepper

2 cups grated Parmesan cheese

8 ounces fettuccine noodles, cooked and drained

1. In a medium saucepan, bring the cream and butter to a light simmer over medium heat.

2. Add the garlic, salt, and pepper and whisk for 30 seconds.

3. Remove the pan from the heat and whisk in the Parmesan cheese until it has fully melted and the sauce is smooth.

4. If the sauce is too thick, whisk in 2 tablespoons of milk at a time until it reaches your desired consistency.

5. Serve the Alfredo sauce over the cooked fettuccine.

Recipe Remix: Turn this creamy Alfredo sauce into a tomato blush sauce by adding 1 cup jarred marinara sauce. Stir the marinara sauce into the Alfredo sauce during step 2 and whisk until it's fully combined. Continue with the recipe as directed.

Ravioli Lasagna

Serves 6

Prep time: 10 minutes • **Cook time:** 45 minutes • **Total time:** 55 minutes

Hot Plate/Stove   Oven

5 or Fewer Ingredients, Cheap Eat, Worth the Wait

Ravioli Lasagna is a fun twist on the classic casserole. Instead of noodles, this recipe uses ravioli, either cheese or meat filled. The ravioli are layered with sauce, beef, and gooey mozzarella cheese to build a hearty dish everyone will love.

Nonstick cooking spray

1 pound ground beef

1 teaspoon salt

½ teaspoon ground black pepper

1 (28-ounce) jar marinara sauce, divided

1 (25-ounce) package frozen ravioli, either meat or cheese filled

1½ cups shredded part-skim mozzarella cheese, divided

¼ cup grated Parmesan cheese

1. Preheat the oven to 400°F. Spray a 13-by-9-inch baking dish with nonstick cooking spray.

2. Heat a large skillet over medium-high heat. Put the ground beef into the skillet and season it with salt and pepper.

3. Cook the beef for 5 to 7 minutes, stirring and breaking it into smaller pieces as it cooks. When the beef is cooked through and no longer pink, remove the pan from the heat and drain off the fat.

4. Pour one-third of the jar of marinara sauce into the bottom of the baking dish and spread it into an even layer.

5. Arrange half of the frozen ravioli and half of the cooked ground beef on top of the sauce. Top with ½ cup of the mozzarella cheese.

6. Repeat the layering process by adding one-third of the jar of sauce, the remaining half of the ravioli, the remaining half of the ground beef, and ½ cup of the mozzarella cheese.

7. Top with the remaining third of the marinara sauce and the remaining ½ cup mozzarella cheese. Sprinkle the Parmesan cheese over the top.

8. Cover the baking dish with aluminum foil and bake for 40 to 45 minutes, or until the ravioli are cooked and the casserole is heated through.

Make It Yourself: To make homemade marinara sauce, heat 1 tablespoon olive oil in a large pot over medium-high heat. Add a diced medium onion to the pot and sauté for 5 minutes. Add 4 minced garlic cloves and stir for 30 seconds. Add 2 (28-ounce) cans tomato puree, 3 tablespoons Italian seasoning, 2 teaspoons salt, and ½ teaspoon ground black pepper and stir until combined. Bring the sauce to a vigorous simmer, then reduce the heat to low and cook the sauce at a slow simmer for 20 minutes. Remove the pot from the heat and stir in ¼ cup grated Parmesan cheese.

Crispy Oven "Fried" Chicken

Serves 4

Prep time: 10 minutes • **Cook time:** 25 minutes • **Total time:** 35 minutes

◻ Oven

Cheap Eat, Healthy

Crispy Oven "Fried" Chicken is a clever way to get a crispy texture without the added fat from deep-frying. Chicken breasts are dredged in pulverized, seasoned cornflakes and then baked until crispy. You can also try this method with thinly sliced, boneless pork chops or cube steak instead of chicken.

Nonstick cooking spray

4 thinly sliced boneless, skinless chicken cutlets

1 teaspoon salt

¼ teaspoon ground black pepper

1 large egg

2 tablespoons milk

2 cups cornflakes, crushed

½ teaspoon garlic powder

½ teaspoon onion powder

¼ teaspoon cayenne

2 tablespoons unsalted butter, melted

1. Preheat the oven to 350°F. Line a baking sheet with foil and place an oven-safe baking rack on top of the foil. Spray the baking rack with non-stick cooking spray.

2. Season both sides of the chicken with the salt and pepper.

3. In a small, shallow bowl, whisk together the egg and milk.

4. In a separate small, shallow bowl, combine the cornflakes, garlic powder, onion powder, and cayenne.

5. Dip the chicken into the egg mixture, ensuring both sides are completely covered. Then, dredge the chicken in the cornflake mixture and press the crushed cornflakes onto the chicken. Flip the chicken and coat the other side.

6. Place the coated chicken on the prepared baking sheet. Repeat with the remaining pieces of chicken.

7. Drizzle the melted butter over the coated chicken.

8. Bake for 20 to 25 minutes, or until the chicken reaches an internal temperature of 165°F.

Recipe Remix: Mix up the flavor of this recipe by adding 2 teaspoons of taco seasoning, Caribbean jerk seasoning, Creole seasoning, or five-spice seasoning instead of the garlic powder, onion, powder, and cayenne.

Baked Ham and Cheese Sliders

Serves 6

Prep time: 5 minutes • **Cook time:** 26 minutes • **Total time:** 31 minutes

Microwave Oven

Cheap Eat

Sliders are mini versions of classic sandwiches. These ham and cheese sliders are made with sweetened rolls and are coated in a flavorful sauce then baked until they are golden and the cheese has melted. They're perfect for sharing, so invite your friends and dig in.

Nonstick cooking spray

1 (12-count) package Hawaiian sweet rolls

¾ pound cooked deli ham, thinly sliced, divided

¾ pound Swiss cheese, thinly sliced

½ cup butter

1 tablespoon Dijon mustard

1 tablespoon poppy seeds

2 teaspoons onion powder

2 teaspoons Worcester- shire sauce

½ teaspoon salt

¼ teaspoon ground black pepper

1. Preheat the oven to 350°F. Line a 13-by-9-inch baking dish with aluminum foil and spray the foil with nonstick cooking spray.

2. Remove the rolls from the package, but do not separate them. Using a serrated knife, cut the rolls in half crosswise, through the center.

3. Lay the bottom portion of the rolls in the prepared baking dish, cut-side up.

4. Arrange half of the ham in an even layer on top of the rolls.

5. Place the cheese in an even layer on top of the ham.

6. Add the remaining ham in an even layer on top of the cheese and place the top portion of the rolls, cut-side down.

7. In a small microwave-safe bowl, melt the butter in the microwave on HIGH (100% power) for 1 minute.

8. Carefully remove the bowl from the microwave and whisk in the Dijon mustard, poppy seeds, onion powder, Worcestershire sauce, salt, and pepper.

9. Carefully pour the butter mixture over the rolls. Spread the mixture with a spatula to ensure all of the rolls are evenly coated.

10. Cover the baking dish with aluminum foil and allow the sliders to sit for 5 minutes.

11. Leave the foil cover on and bake for 20 minutes, or until the cheese has melted.

12. Remove the foil cover and bake for 3 to 5 minutes more, or until the rolls are lightly golden.

Recipe Remix: Turn these into Turkey Ranch Sliders by substituting deli turkey for the deli ham, American cheese for the Swiss cheese, and ranch salad dressing for the Dijon mustard.

Brown Sugar Garlic Pork Medallions

Serves 6

Prep time: 10 minutes • **Cook time:** 12 minutes • **Total time:** 22 minutes

Hot Plate/Stove   Oven

Cheap Eat

This pork dish may look fancy and is sure to impress, but the recipe is easy to make. You can even use boneless, skinless chicken breast instead of the pork, if you wish. With chicken, make sure the internal temperature reaches 165°F before eating.

1 boneless pork
   tenderloin

1 teaspoon salt

¼ teaspoon ground
   black pepper

3 tablespoons unsalted
   butter, divided

6 garlic cloves, minced

¼ cup brown sugar,
   packed

1 tablespoon honey

½ teaspoon Italian
   seasoning blend

⅛ teaspoon crushed
   red pepper flakes

1. Preheat the oven to 400°F.

2. Season the pork tenderloin all over with salt and black pepper.

3. Cut the seasoned pork tenderloin into ½-inch-thick pieces or medallions.

4. In a large ovenproof skillet, melt 2 tablespoons of the butter over medium-high heat.

5. Put the pork medallions into the skillet and sear them for 2 to 3 minutes on each side, or until golden brown. Remove the seared medallions from the skillet and let them rest on a plate.

6. Put the remaining tablespoon of butter into the skillet and let it melt.

7. Add the garlic and cook for about 30 seconds, stirring frequently, until fragrant. Remove the skillet from heat.

8. Stir in the brown sugar, honey, Italian seasoning blend, and crushed red pepper.

9. Return the pork medallions to the skillet.

10. Place the skillet in the oven and roast for 10 to 15 minutes, or until they reach an internal temperature of 145°F.

Smart Shopping: Pork tenderloin is usually sold two to a package, making it easy to split the cost with a roommate. Freeze any extra pork in a zip-top bag for up to six months, making sure to remove any excess air before sealing.

Microwave BBQ Chicken Nachos

Serves 4

Prep time: 5 minutes • **Cook time:** 3 minutes • **Total time:** 8 minutes

▢ Microwave

15 Minutes, 5 or Fewer Ingredients, Cheap Eat, Healthy

These BBQ Chicken Nachos are like a deconstructed taco. Crispy tortilla chips are piled high with chicken, BBQ sauce, and cheese, then cooked to crispy perfection in the microwave. These are perfect for watching the big game with friends. You can easily swap out the BBQ sauce for hot wing sauce, honey mustard, or your favorite sauce.

2 (12.5-ounce) cans canned chicken breast, drained

⅓ cup barbecue sauce

4 cups tortilla chips

1½ cups shredded cheddar cheese

½ cup thinly sliced scallions

Sour cream, guacamole, or pico de gallo, for topping (optional)

1. In a medium bowl, combine the chicken and barbecue sauce.

2. Place the tortilla chips in a large microwave-safe baking dish and top with the barbecue chicken.

3. Top with the cheddar cheese and scallions.

4. Microwave on HIGH (100% power) for 2 to 3 minutes, or until the cheese has melted.

5. Top with your favorite nacho toppings.

Smart Shopping: For this recipe, try buying cheddar cheese in block form and grate it yourself. Not only is it more affordable, but block cheese also melts better than the pre-shredded varieties because there aren't as many preservatives in it.

Microwave Meat Loaf

Serves 6

Prep time: 5 minutes • **Cook time:** 15 minutes, plus 10 minutes to rest
Total time: 30 minutes

▢ **Microwave**

Cheap Eat

Meat loaf is a classic American recipe. This microwave version is quicker than the traditional oven version but is just as tasty.

1 large egg, lightly beaten

5 tablespoons ketchup, divided

1 sleeve saltine crackers, crushed

2 teaspoons garlic power

2 teaspoons onion powder

2 teaspoons dried minced onions

½ teaspoon salt

¼ teaspoon ground black pepper

1 pound ground beef

2 tablespoons brown sugar

1. In a large bowl, combine the egg and 2 tablespoons of the ketchup with the cracker crumbs, garlic powder, onion powder, dried minced onion, salt, and pepper.

2. Add the beef and mix well.

3. Using your hands, shape the beef into an oval loaf and place it in a shallow medium microwave-safe dish.

4. Cover with plastic wrap and microwave on HIGH (100% power) for 10 to 12 minutes, or until the internal temperature of the beef reaches 160°F. Drain off any excess fat.

5. While the meat loaf is cooking, in a small bowl, combine the remaining 3 tablespoons of ketchup and the brown sugar.

6. Spread the ketchup glaze over the meat loaf.

7. Replace the plastic wrap cover and microwave on HIGH for 2 to 3 minutes, or until heated through.

8. Allow the meat loaf to rest for 10 minutes before slicing.

Miso-Glazed Salmon

Serves 4

Prep time: 5 minutes, plus 30 minutes to marinate • **Cook time:** 10 minutes
Total time: 45 minutes

▭ Oven

5 or Fewer Ingredients, Worth the Wait

This elegant yet easy meal takes only 10 minutes to cook but be sure to plan ahead. It needs to marinate for 30 minutes before broiling. Serve this salmon atop a bed of rice with your favorite steamed vegetable on the side.

3 tablespoons white miso

2 tablespoons sake

2 tablespoons granu-
lated sugar

2 teaspoons soy sauce

4 (6-ounce) skinless salmon fillets

Nonstick cooking spray

1. In a small bowl, whisk together the miso, sake, sugar, and soy sauce.

2. Place the salmon fillets into a container with a tight-fitting lid, or a zip-top bag. Pour the marinade over the salmon, making sure it is completely coated. Marinate in the refrigerator for 30 minutes.

3. When the salmon has marinated and is ready to cook, adjust an oven rack so it is 8 inches below the broiler and preheat the oven to broil.

4. Line a rimmed baking sheet with aluminum foil and spray the foil with nonstick cooking spray.

5. Place the marinated salmon fillets on the baking sheet, and place the baking sheet in the oven on the oven rack 8 inches below the broiler.

6. Broil for 8 to 10 minutes, or until the salmon easily flakes.

7. If the top of the salmon starts to char and it hasn't finished cooking yet, move the salmon to a lower rack in the oven and continue cooking until the salmon is cooked through.

Chocolate Caramel Sundae, page 127

CHAPTER 8

DESSERTS

Microwave Chocolate Chip Cookie 120

Chocolate Peanut Butter Mug Cake 121

Banana Bread in a Mug 122

5-Minute Apple Crisp 123

No-Bake Cheesecake 124

Brownie for One 125

Banana Pudding Parfait 126

Chocolate Caramel Sundae 127

Crispy Rice Bars 128

Cinnamon Roll-Ups 129

Microwave Chocolate Chip Cookie

Serves 1

Prep time: 5 minutes • **Cook time:** 1 minute • **Total time:** 6 minutes

☐ Microwave

15 Minutes, Cheap Eat, Vegetarian

There is nothing like a warm chocolate chip cookie to make you feel warm and cozy. This easy microwave version gives you the same comfort without the wait. Pour yourself a tall glass of your favorite milk and dig in.

1 tablespoon unsalted butter

1 tablespoon granulated sugar

1 tablespoon firmly packed brown sugar

3 drops vanilla extract

Pinch salt

1 egg yolk

Scant ¼ cup flour

2 heaping tablespoons semisweet chocolate chips

1. In a microwave-safe mug, melt the butter in the microwave on HIGH (100% power) for 15 to 30 seconds.

2. Add the granulated sugar, brown sugar, vanilla extract, and salt to the melted butter. Stir to combine.

3. Separate the egg yolk from the white. Add the yolk to the mixture in the mug, discarding the white (or saving it for another recipe). Stir until the yolk is fully incorporated.

4. Add the flour to the mug and stir until just combined.

5. Stir in the chocolate chips.

6. Microwave on HIGH for 40 seconds, then check for doneness by inserting a toothpick into the center of the cookie. If the toothpick comes out clean, the cookie is done.

7. If it comes out with batter on it, continue to microwave in 10-second increments, testing for doneness after each increment. Do not cook for more than 60 seconds. The cookie will continue to cook as it cools.

Chocolate Peanut Butter Mug Cake

Serves 1

Prep time: 5 minutes • **Cook time:** 3 minutes • **Total time:** 8 minutes

▫ Microwave

15 Minutes, Cheap Eat, Vegetarian

Chocolate and peanut butter are a classic flavor combination. Whether you're studying or hanging out with friends, this delicious microwave mug cake is sure to satisfy your chocolate craving.

2 tablespoons unsalted butter

2 tablespoons peanut butter

2 tablespoons sugar

½ teaspoon vanilla

1 egg

3 tablespoons unsweetened cocoa powder

2 tablespoons flour

⅛ teaspoon salt

⅛ teaspoon baking powder

3 tablespoons semisweet chocolate chips

1. In a small microwave-safe bowl, melt the butter in the microwave on HIGH (100% power) for 15 to 30 seconds. Then, stir in the peanut butter.

2. In a microwave-safe mug, combine the sugar, vanilla, and egg.

3. In a separate small bowl, combine the cocoa powder, flour, salt, and baking powder.

4. Add the flour mixture to the mug with the sugar and egg mixture and stir until combined.

5. Add the peanut butter and melted butter mixture to the mug and stir until combined.

6. Add the chocolate chips and stir until combined.

7. Microwave on HIGH for 1 to 2 minutes. Check for doneness by inserting a toothpick into the center of the cake. If the toothpick comes out clean, the cake is done. If it comes out with batter on it, continue to microwave in 10-second increments, testing for doneness after each increment.

Make It Yourself: Don't have cocoa powder? No problem! Put ½ cup semisweet chocolate chips into a blender or food processor and pulse to form a powder. If using this substitution, omit 1 tablespoon of butter.

Banana Bread in a Mug

Serves 1

Prep time: 5 minutes • **Cook time:** 3 minutes • **Total time:** 8 minutes

🔲 Microwave

15 Minutes, Cheap Eat, Vegetarian

Banana bread is one of those recipes that reminds people of the comforts of home. For a sweeter and stronger banana flavor, use overripe bananas that are starting to turn black on the outside. This recipe is the perfect way to use up bananas that have been hanging around for a while.

Nonstick cooking spray

3 tablespoons flour

1 tablespoon granulated sugar

2 tablespoons brown sugar

⅛ teaspoon salt

⅛ teaspoon baking powder

⅛ teaspoon baking soda

1 egg

¼ teaspoon vanilla extract

1 tablespoon canola oil

1 tablespoon milk

1 very ripe banana, mashed

1. Spray the inside of a microwave-safe mug with nonstick cooking spray.

2. In the same mug, combine the flour, granulated sugar, brown sugar, salt, baking powder, and baking soda.

3. Add the egg and stir until it is incorporated into the dry ingredients.

4. Stir in the vanilla, canola oil, milk, and mashed banana.

5. Microwave on HIGH (100% power) for 2 to 3 minutes. Check for doneness by inserting a toothpick into the center of the bread. If the toothpick comes out clean, the bread is done. If it comes out with batter on it, continue to microwave in 15-second increments, testing for doneness after each increment.

Smart Shopping: You don't have to buy bananas by the bunch. If you only need one or two, choose the exact ones you want at the grocery store. For this recipe, look for the ripest banana.

5-Minute Apple Crisp

Serves 1

Prep time: 5 minute • **Cook time:** 4 minutes • **Total time:** 9 minutes

▢ Microwave

15 Minutes, Cheap Eat, Vegetarian

There is something magical about warm apple crisp. It's the perfect combination of sweet, tender fruit topped with a crispy oat layer. This recipe can be made in under 10 minutes, so it's the perfect quick after-dinner treat or late-night study snack. Serve it with a big scoop of vanilla ice cream.

1½ tablespoons unsalted butter

2 tablespoons quick oats

1 tablespoon chopped pecans

1¼ tablespoons flour, divided

1¼ tablespoons brown sugar, divided

¼ teaspoon ground cinnamon, divided

Pinch salt

1 cup peeled chopped apples

1. In a small microwave-safe bowl, melt the butter in the microwave on HIGH (100% power) for 30 seconds.

2. Stir in the oats, pecans, 1 tablespoon of the flour, 1 tablespoon of the brown sugar, and ⅛ teaspoon of the cinnamon.

3. Put the chopped apples into a small bowl. Add the remaining ¾ teaspoons of flour, ¾ teaspoons of brown sugar, and ⅛ teaspoon of cinnamon to the apples and stir until combined.

4. Put 1 tablespoon of the oat mixture in the bottom of a microwave-safe mug. Top with the apple mixture and then with the remaining oat mixture.

5. Microwave on HIGH for 3 minutes and 30 seconds.

6. Allow the apple crisp to cool for a few minutes before eating.

Recipe Remix: This recipe works great with many different fruits. Try substituting the same amount of chopped, peeled peaches; chopped, peeled pears; blueberries; or raspberries for the chopped apples.

No-Bake Cheesecake

Serves 1

Prep time: 10 minutes, plus 20 minutes to chill • **Total time:** 30 minutes

No Cook

Cheap Eat, Vegetarian

Traditional cheesecakes are delicious, but they can be fussy and time consuming to make. This quick and easy no-bake version will give you the flavors you're craving without the work. Make a double batch of this and save the extra portion for another time. Store it in an airtight container in the refrigerator for up to 4 days.

2 full-size graham crackers

1 tablespoon unsalted butter, melted

Pinch salt

2 ounces cream cheese, softened

2 tablespoons granulated sugar

½ teaspoon vanilla extract

½ cup frozen whipped topping, thawed

1. Put the graham crackers into a zip-top bag. Using a rolling pin, skillet, or a canned good, crush them into fine crumbs.

2. In a small microwave-safe bowl, combine the butter and salt. Microwave them on HIGH (100% power) for 30 seconds, or until the butter has melted.

3. Add the crushed graham crackers to the melted butter and stir until combined. The mixture should resemble wet sand.

4. Transfer the graham cracker crumbs to a serving bowl.

5. In a separate small bowl, combine the cream cheese, granulated sugar, and vanilla. Mix well. Then, fold in the whipped topping.

6. Spoon the cream cheese mixture on top of the graham cracker crumbs.

7. Refrigerate for at least 20 minutes before serving.

Smart Shopping: Buy whipped cream cheese instead of regular cream cheese to make it easier to incorporate.

Brownie for One

Serves 1

Prep time: 5 minutes • **Cook time:** 2 minutes • **Total time:** 7 minutes

Microwave

15 Minutes, Cheap Eat, Vegetarian

There is nothing like a warm, rich brownie to satisfy a chocolate craving. This decadent, fudgy treat can be made in under 10 minutes. You can take this recipe to the next level by serving it with ice cream, a drizzle of hot fudge, whipped cream, and a cherry! Grab a spoon and enjoy.

¼ **cup flour**

¼ **cup unsweetened cocoa powder**

3 **tablespoons dark brown sugar**

Pinch salt

⅓ **cup milk**

2 **tablespoons canola oil**

½ **teaspoon vanilla extract**

1 **tablespoon semisweet chocolate chips**

1. In a microwave-safe mug, mix together the flour, cocoa powder, brown sugar, and salt.

2. Stir in the milk, canola oil, and vanilla.

3. Stir in the chocolate chips.

4. Microwave on HIGH (100% power) for 1 to 2 minutes. Check for doneness by inserting a toothpick into the center of the brownie. If the toothpick comes out clean, the brownie is done. If it comes out with batter on it, continue to microwave in 15-second increments, testing for doneness after each increment.

Make It Even Faster: Prep ahead by mixing up this recipe, covering it with plastic wrap, and stashing it in the fridge for up to 24 hours. When you get a craving, simply remove the plastic wrap, and microwave as directed in step 4.

Banana Pudding Parfait

Serves 1

Prep time: 5 minutes • **Total time:** 5 minutes

No Cook

15 Minutes, 5 or Fewer Ingredients, Cheap Eat, Vegetarian

This easy parfait has layers of crispy vanilla cookies, creamy pudding, and, of course, sweet bananas. The best part about this dessert is digging your spoon into the bowl, so you get a bit of each layer in every perfect bite.

6 vanilla wafers

1 medium banana

1 (5.5-ounce) container vanilla pudding

2 tablespoons frozen whipped topping, thawed

1. Place the vanilla wafers in a zip-top bag and seal it. Using a rolling pin, skillet, or canned good, crush the wafers into crumbs. Reserve 1 teaspoon of the cookie crumbs and set aside.

2. Cut the banana into slices. Reserve 2 banana slices.

3. Place half of the cookie crumbs into a small glass or serving bowl. Place half of the bananas on top.

4. Spoon half of the pudding on top of the bananas.

5. Repeat the layering process with the remaining cookie crumbs, bananas, and pudding.

6. Top with the whipped topping, reserved banana slices, and reserved cookie crumbs.

Recipe Remix: Make an Elvis-inspired parfait by adding peanut butter and Microwave Bacon (page 44). Put 2 tablespoons of peanut butter into a microwave-safe bowl and microwave it on HIGH (100% power) for 30 seconds, or until it thins out. Crumble the bacon into small pieces. Prepare the recipe as directed until step 4. After adding the bananas, drizzle half of the warm peanut butter over the bananas and add half of the bacon crumbles. Repeat this in step 5. Finish the recipe as directed.

Chocolate Caramel Sundae

Serves 1

Prep time: 5 minutes • **Total time:** 5 minutes

No Cook

15 Minutes, 5 or Fewer Ingredients, Cheap Eat, Vegetarian

Sometimes nothing will satisfy your sweet tooth like a big old ice cream sundae. This sundae is layered with decadent chocolate and sweet, salty caramel—the perfect combination. Of course, you can pile on any of your favorite sundae toppings such as chopped peanuts, banana slices, or sprinkles.

3 scoops salted caramel ice cream

2 tablespoons hot fudge sauce

2 tablespoons caramel sauce

Whipped cream

1 maraschino cherry

1. Scoop the ice cream into a bowl.

2. Put the hot fudge sauce in a small, microwave-safe bowl. Microwave on HIGH (100% power) for 10 to 15 seconds, until the fudge sauce is hot and pourable.

3. Drizzle the hot fudge sauce and caramel sauce over the ice cream.

4. Top with whipped cream and a maraschino cherry.

Recipe Remix: Turn this into a Stroopwafels Sundae! Stroopwafels are thin, Dutch caramel-filled wafers. Scoop three scoops of salted caramel ice cream into a bowl. Chop one large stroopwafel wafer into small, bite-sized pieces, reserving 1 tablespoon for topping. Sprinkle the stroopwafel pieces on top of the ice cream. Drizzle two tablespoons of caramel sauce over the wafers and top with whipped cream. Sprinkle the reserved stroopwafel pieces on top.

Crispy Rice Bars

Serves 1

Prep time: 5 minutes • **Cook time:** 1 minute • **Total time:** 6 minutes

▢ Microwave

15 Minutes, 5 or Fewer Ingredients, Cheap Eat

These Crispy Rice Bars are reminiscent of a classic childhood treat. They're crispy, gooey, and altogether delicious. But, most importantly, they are super easy to whip up. The trick to getting soft, gooey treats is to not overcook the marshmallows. When heating the marshmallows, keep a close eye on them and remove from the microwave as soon as they start puffing up.

½ **tablespoon unsalted butter**

1 cup miniature marshmallows, or 6 large marshmallows

Pinch salt

1 cup crispy rice cereal

Nonstick cooking spray

1. In a large microwave-safe bowl, melt the butter in the microwave on HIGH (100% power) for 15 seconds.

2. Add the marshmallows to the bowl and microwave on HIGH for 30 seconds, or until the marshmallows puff up.

3. Add the salt and stir until it's incorporated.

4. Stir in the crispy rice cereal until it is well coated with the marshmallows.

5. Spray a sheet of parchment paper with nonstick cooking spray. Transfer the mixture to the parchment paper.

6. Spray your hands with nonstick cooking spray to keep the mixture from sticking to your hands and then shape the mixture into a bar shape.

7. Cool completely before eating.

Recipe Remix: Try using your favorite cereal in place of the crispy rice cereal. Some of my favorites include frosted graham cracker cereal, fruity rice cereal, and strawberry-flavored checkered rice cereal.

Cinnamon Roll-Ups

Serves 1

Prep time: 5 minutes • **Cook time:** 15 minutes • **Total time:** 20 minutes

⬛ Oven

Cheap Eat, Vegetarian

These sweet roll-ups make a great snack or breakfast on the go. Sweetened cream cheese is enveloped in soft bread, dredged in a cinnamon-sugar mixture and then baked to perfection.

2 slices white sandwich bread

2 tablespoons cream cheese, at room temperature

2½ teaspoons powdered sugar

Drop vanilla extract

3 teaspoons granulated sugar

Pinch ground cinnamon

2½ teaspoons butter, melted

1. Preheat the oven to 350°F.

2. Trim the crusts off the bread. Flatten the bread slices with a rolling pin or canned good wrapped in plastic wrap.

3. In a small bowl, mix together the cream cheese, powdered sugar, and vanilla.

4. On a small plate, combine the granulated sugar and cinnamon, and mix until combined. Set aside.

5. Spread 1 tablespoon of the cream cheese mixture on one end of the bread slice.

6. Starting at the end with the cream cheese mixture, roll up the bread.

7. Dip the bread roll in melted butter, then roll it in the cinnamon-sugar mixture until it is fully coated. Place the coated roll on a rimmed baking sheet.

8. Repeat steps 5 through 7 with the remaining bread slice.

9. Bake the rolls for 15 minutes, or until golden brown.

Smart Shopping: Look for smaller, one-pound canisters of sugar that are perfect for college kitchens.

Measurement Conversions

OVEN TEMPERATURES

FAHRENHEIT	CELSIUS (APPROXIMATE)
250°F	120°C
300°F	150°C
325°F	165°C
350°F	180°C
375°F	190°C
400°F	200°C
425°F	220°C
450°F	230°C

VOLUME EQUIVALENTS (LIQUID)

US STANDARD	US STANDARD (OUNCES)	METRIC (APPROXIMATE)
2 tablespoons	1 fl. oz.	30 mL
¼ cup	2 fl. oz.	60 mL
½ cup	4 fl. oz.	120 mL
1 cup	8 fl. oz.	240 mL
1½ cups	12 fl. oz.	355 mL
2 cups or 1 pint	16 fl. oz.	475 mL
4 cups or 1 quart	32 fl. oz.	1 L
1 gallon	128 fl. oz.	4 L

WEIGHT EQUIVALENTS

US STANDARD	METRIC (APPROXIMATE)
½ ounce	15 g
1 ounce	30 g
2 ounces	60 g
4 ounces	115 g
8 ounces	225 g
12 ounces	340 g
16 ounces or 1 pound	455 g

VOLUME EQUIVALENTS (DRY)

US STANDARD	METRIC (APPROXIMATE)
⅛ teaspoon	0.5 mL
¼ teaspoon	1 mL
½ teaspoon	2 mL
¾ teaspoon	4 mL
1 teaspoon	5 mL
1 tablespoon	15 mL
¼ cup	59 mL
⅓ cup	79 mL
½ cup	118 mL
⅔ cup	156 mL
¾ cup	177 mL
1 cup	235 mL
2 cups or 1 pint	475 mL
3 cups	700 mL
4 cups or 1 quart	1 L

HOT
Wasabi
Flavored
Peas

WASABI FLAVORED GREEN PEAS

NET WT. 9.90 OZ (280g)

Resources

FoodWasteAlliance.org: To learn more about food waste and how you can help minimize food waste

ItIsaKeeper.com: For easy recipes using easy-to-find-ingredients

Nutrition.gov: To learn about making healthful eating choices

USDA.gov: For comprehensive nutrition and food safety resources

Index

A

Almond Overnight Oats,
Strawberry, 39
Apples
  Apple Cranberry Yogurt
    Salad, 68
  5-Minute Apple Crisp, 123
  Microwave Apple Cinnamon
    Oatmeal, 38
  Warm Apple Pie Dip, 52
Avocados
  BLT Avocado Toast, 42
  Classic Guacamole, 55
  Tuna Salad Avocado Bowls, 72

B

Bacon
  Bacon and Blue Cheese
    Wedge Salad, 67
  BLT Avocado Toast, 42
  Microwave Bacon, 44
Bananas
  Banana Bread in a
    Mug, 122
  Banana Granola Bites, 60
  Banana Pudding Parfait, 126
BBQ Chicken Nachos,
  Microwave, 114
Beans
  Bean and Cheese
    Quesadillas, 85
  Southwest Black Bean
    Soup, 99
  Vegetarian Burrito
    Bowls, 86
  Vegetarian Chili, 87
Beef
  Microwave Meat Loaf, 115
  The Perfect Burger, 95
  Ultimate Roast Beef
    Sandwiches, 80

Berries
  Apple Cranberry Yogurt
    Salad, 68
  Blueberry Pancake
    in a Mug, 40
  Brussels Sprouts
    Cranberry Salad, 69
  Strawberry Almond
    Overnight Oats, 39
  Strawberry Pecan
    Quinoa Salad, 66
"Best by" dates, 13
Blenders, 8, 29
  Creamy Hummus, 56
  Mocha Smoothie, 37
Blueberry Pancake in a
  Mug, 40
Blue Cheese Wedge Salad,
  Bacon and, 67
Boiling, 9, 29
Bowls
  Tuna Salad Avocado Bowls, 72
  Vegetarian Burrito Bowls, 86
Breakfasts
  BLT Avocado Toast, 42
  Blueberry Pancake
    in a Mug, 40
  Chewy Chocolate Chip
    Granola Bars, 36
  French Toast in a Mug, 41
  Microwave Apple Cinnamon
    Oatmeal, 38
  Microwave Bacon, 44
  Microwave Scrambled Eggs, 43
  Mocha Smoothie, 37
  Sausage and Egg Breakfast
    Taquitos, 45
  Strawberry Almond
    Overnight Oats, 39
Broccoli Salad, Nutty, 71
Brownie for One, 125

Brown Sugar Garlic Pork
  Medallions, 112–113
Brussels Sprouts Cranberry
  Salad, 69
Buffalo Chicken Flatbreads, 81
Burger, The Perfect, 95
Burrito Bowls, Vegetarian, 86

C

Cake, Chocolate Peanut
  Butter Mug, 121
Caprese Chicken Grilled Cheese
  Sandwiches, 78–79
Caramel
  Chocolate Caramel Sundae, 127
  S'mores Caramel Popcorn, 58
Cheap eats
  Baked Chicken Tenders, 94
  Baked Ham and Cheese
    Sliders, 110–111
  Banana Bread in a Mug, 122
  Banana Granola Bites, 60
  Banana Pudding Parfait, 126
  Bean and Cheese
    Quesadillas, 85
  Blueberry Pancake
    in a Mug, 40
  Brownie for One, 125
  Chewy Chocolate Chip
    Granola Bars, 36
  Chicken Caesar Wraps, 76
  Chocolate Caramel
    Sundae, 127
  Chocolate Peanut Butter
    Mug Cake, 121
  Cinnamon Roll-Ups, 129
  Cinnamon Tortilla Crisps, 50
  Classic Guacamole, 55
  Cookie Dough Dip, 53
  Creamy Fettuccine Alfredo, 105
  Creamy Hummus, 56

Cheap eats *(continued)*

Crispy Oven "Fried"
Chicken, 108–109
Crispy Rice Bars, 128
Everything Bagel Potato
Chips, 48–49
5-Minute Apple Crisp, 123
French Toast in a Mug, 41
Italian Pork Chops, 96–97
Lemon Pepper Tuna
Lettuce Wraps, 74
Loaded Baked Potatoes, 90
Microwave Apple Cinnamon
Oatmeal, 38
Microwave BBQ Chicken
Nachos, 114
Microwave Chicken
Enchiladas, 92
Microwave Chocolate
Chip Cookie, 120
Microwave Granola, 59
Microwave Kettle Corn, 57
Microwave Mac & Cheese, 91
Microwave Meat Loaf, 115
Microwave Risotto, 89
Microwave Scrambled Eggs, 43
Microwave Spaghetti
Marinara, 104
Mini Pepperoni Pizzas, 63
Mocha Smoothie, 37
No-Bake Cheesecake, 124
The Perfect Burger, 95
Pineapple Salsa, 54
Ravioli Lasagna, 106–107
Sesame Ramen Salad, 70
Shawarma Roasted
Chickpeas, 61
S'mores Caramel Popcorn, 58
Southwest Black Bean
Soup, 99
Spicy Wasabi Trail Mix, 62
Spinach Pesto Flatbread
Pizzas, 84
Strawberry Almond
Overnight Oats, 39
Tuna Salad Avocado Bowls, 72

Turkey Club Wraps, 75
Two-Ingredient Veggie Dip, 51
Vegetarian Chili, 87
Veggie Gyros, 73
Veggie Ramen, 88
Warm Apple Pie Dip, 52
Cheese
Bacon and Blue Cheese
Wedge Salad, 67
Baked Ham and Cheese
Sliders, 110–111
Bean and Cheese
Quesadillas, 85
Caprese Chicken Grilled
Cheese Sandwiches, 78–79
Microwave Mac & Cheese, 91
Microwave Parmesan
Chicken, 93
Cheesecake, No-Bake, 124
Chicken
Baked Chicken Tenders, 94
Buffalo Chicken Flatbreads, 81
Caprese Chicken Grilled
Cheese Sandwiches, 78–79
Chicken Caesar Wraps, 76
Crispy Oven "Fried"
Chicken, 108–109
Microwave BBQ Chicken
Nachos, 114
Microwave Chicken
Enchiladas, 92
Microwave Parmesan
Chicken, 93
Chickpeas
Creamy Hummus, 56
Shawarma Roasted
Chickpeas, 61
Chips, Everything Bagel
Potato, 48–49
Chocolate
Chewy Chocolate Chip
Granola Bars, 36
Chocolate Caramel Sundae, 127
Chocolate Peanut Butter
Mug Cake, 121

Cookie Dough Dip, 53
Microwave Chocolate
Chip Cookie, 120
Mocha Smoothie, 37
S'mores Caramel
Popcorn, 58
Chopping, 9, 22
Cinnamon
Cinnamon Roll-Ups, 129
Cinnamon Tortilla Crisps, 50
Microwave Apple Cinnamon
Oatmeal, 38
Cod, Lemony, 98
Cookie, Microwave
Chocolate Chip, 120
Cookie Dough Dip, 53
Cooking
terminology, 8–9
tips, 4–5
Cranberries
Apple Cranberry Yogurt
Salad, 68
Brussels Sprouts
Cranberry Salad, 69

D

Desserts
Banana Bread in a Mug, 122
Banana Pudding Parfait, 126
Brownie for One, 125
Chocolate Caramel
Sundae, 127
Chocolate Peanut Butter
Mug Cake, 121
Cinnamon Roll-Ups, 129
Cookie Dough Dip, 53
Crispy Rice Bars, 128
5-Minute Apple Crisp, 123
Microwave Chocolate
Chip Cookie, 120
No-Bake Cheesecake, 124
S'mores Caramel Popcorn, 58
Warm Apple Pie Dip, 52
Dicing, 9, 22
Dining halls, 12

Dips and spreads
  Classic Guacamole, 55
  Cookie Dough Dip, 53
  Creamy Hummus, 56
  Pineapple Salsa, 54
  Two-Ingredient Veggie Dip, 51
  Warm Apple Pie Dip, 52
Dividing, 9
Dredging, 9

E

Eggs
  Microwave Scrambled Eggs, 43
  Sausage and Egg Breakfast
    Taquitos, 45
Enchiladas, Microwave
    Chicken, 92
Equipment, 8
Everything Bagel Potato
    Chips, 48–49

F

15 minutes
  Apple Cranberry Yogurt
    Salad, 68
  Bacon and Blue Cheese
    Wedge Salad, 67
  Banana Bread in a Mug, 122
  Banana Granola Bites, 60
  Banana Pudding Parfait, 126
  Bean and Cheese
    Quesadillas, 85
  BLT Avocado Toast, 42
  Blueberry Pancake
    in a Mug, 40
  Brownie for One, 125
  Brussels Sprouts
    Cranberry Salad, 69
  Buffalo Chicken Flatbreads, 81
  Caprese Chicken Grilled
    Cheese Sandwiches, 78–79
  Chicken Caesar Wraps, 76
  Chocolate Caramel Sundae, 127
  Chocolate Peanut Butter
    Mug Cake, 121

Cinnamon Tortilla Crisps, 50
Cobb Salad Pitas, 77
Creamy Fettuccine Alfredo, 105
Creamy Hummus, 56
Crispy Rice Bars, 128
5-Minute Apple Crisp, 123
French Toast in a Mug, 41
Lemon Pepper Tuna
    Lettuce Wraps, 74
Lemony Cod, 98
Loaded Baked Potatoes, 90
Microwave Apple Cinnamon
    Oatmeal, 38
Microwave Bacon, 44
Microwave BBQ Chicken
    Nachos, 114
Microwave Chicken
    Enchiladas, 92
Microwave Chocolate
    Chip Cookie, 120
Microwave Granola, 59
Microwave Kettle Corn, 57
Microwave Mac & Cheese, 91
Microwave Parmesan
    Chicken, 93
Microwave Scrambled Eggs, 43
Mini Pepperoni Pizzas, 63
Mocha Smoothie, 37
Nutty Broccoli Salad, 71
The Perfect Burger, 95
Sesame Ramen Salad, 70
S'mores Caramel Popcorn, 58
Southwest Black Bean
    Soup, 99
Spicy Wasabi Trail Mix, 62
Spinach Pesto Flatbread
    Pizzas, 84
Strawberry Pecan
    Quinoa Salad, 66
Tuna Salad Avocado Bowls, 72
Turkey Club Wraps, 75
Ultimate Roast Beef
    Sandwiches, 80
Vegetarian Burrito Bowls, 86
Vegetarian Chili, 87

Veggie Gyros, 73
Veggie Ramen, 88
Warm Apple Pie Dip, 52
Fish and seafood
  Lemon Pepper Tuna
    Lettuce Wraps, 74
  Lemony Cod, 98
  microwave cooking, 25
  Miso-Glazed Salmon, 116
  toaster oven cooking, 27
  Tuna Salad Avocado Bowls, 72
5 or fewer ingredients
  Apple Cranberry Yogurt
    Salad, 68
  Bacon and Blue Cheese
    Wedge Salad, 67
  Banana Granola Bites, 60
  Banana Pudding Parfait, 126
  Bean and Cheese
    Quesadillas, 85
  BLT Avocado Toast, 42
  Blueberry Pancake
    in a Mug, 40
  Chocolate Caramel Sundae, 127
  Cinnamon Tortilla Crisps, 50
  Creamy Fettuccine Alfredo, 105
  Creamy Hummus, 56
  Crispy Rice Bars, 128
  Everything Bagel Potato
    Chips, 48–49
  Microwave Bacon, 44
  Microwave BBQ Chicken
    Nachos, 114
  Microwave Chicken
    Enchiladas, 92
  Microwave Granola, 59
  Microwave Kettle Corn, 57
  Microwave Mac & Cheese, 91
  Microwave Parmesan
    Chicken, 93
  Microwave Scrambled Eggs, 43
  Microwave Spaghetti
    Marinara, 104
  Mini Pepperoni Pizzas, 63
  Miso-Glazed Salmon, 116

5 or fewer ingredients (*continued*)
  Mocha Smoothie, 37
  Ravioli Lasagna, 106–107
  Sausage and Egg Breakfast
    Taquitos, 45
  Shawarma Roasted
    Chickpeas, 61
  S'mores Caramel Popcorn, 58
  Spicy Wasabi Trail Mix, 62
  Spinach Pesto Flatbread
    Pizzas, 84
  Tuna Salad Avocado
    Bowls, 72
  Two-Ingredient
    Veggie Dip, 51
  Warm Apple Pie Dip, 52
Folding, 20–21
Food storage, 13
French Toast in a Mug, 41
Frying, 29

G
Granola
  Banana Granola Bites, 60
  Chewy Chocolate Chip
    Granola Bars, 36
  Microwave Granola, 59
Grocery shopping, 5
Guacamole, Classic, 55

H
Ham and Cheese Sliders,
  Baked, 110–111
Healthy
  Apple Cranberry Yogurt
    Salad, 68
  Baked Chicken Tenders, 94
  Banana Granola Bites, 60
  Bean and Cheese
    Quesadillas, 85
  Brussels Sprouts
    Cranberry Salad, 69
  Chicken Caesar Wraps, 76
  Classic Guacamole, 55
  Creamy Hummus, 56

Crispy Oven "Fried"
    Chicken, 108–109
  Italian Pork Chops, 96–97
  Lemon Pepper Tuna
    Lettuce Wraps, 74
  Lemony Cod, 98
  Microwave Apple Cinnamon
    Oatmeal, 38
  Microwave BBQ Chicken
    Nachos, 114
  Microwave Granola, 59
  Microwave Parmesan
    Chicken, 93
  Mini Pepperoni Pizzas, 63
  Nutty Broccoli Salad, 71
  Pineapple Salsa, 54
  Shawarma Roasted
    Chickpeas, 61
  Southwest Black Bean
    Soup, 99
  Spinach Pesto Flatbread
    Pizzas, 84
  Strawberry Almond
    Overnight Oats, 39
  Strawberry Pecan
    Quinoa Salad, 66
  Tuna Salad Avocado
    Bowls, 72
  Vegetarian Burrito Bowls, 86
  Vegetarian Chili, 87
  Veggie Gyros, 73
  Zesty Spaghetti Squash
    Salad, 102–103
Hot plates, 8.
    See also Stoves
  Bean and Cheese
    Quesadillas, 85
  Caprese Chicken Grilled
    Cheese Sandwiches, 78–79
  Italian Pork Chops, 96–97
  The Perfect Burger, 95
Hummus, Creamy, 56

I
Ingredient staples, 10–12

K
Knife skills, 21–23

L
Leftovers, 12
Lemon Pepper Tuna
    Lettuce Wraps, 74
Lemony Cod, 98
Lettuce
  BLT Avocado Toast, 42
  Lemon Pepper Tuna
    Lettuce Wraps, 74

M
Meal prepping, 18
Measuring ingredients, 19–20
Meat Loaf, Microwave, 115
Meats. *See also specific*
  microwave cooking, 25
  toaster oven cooking, 27
Menu planning, 14
Microwaves, 8, 25–27
  Baked Ham and Cheese
    Sliders, 110–111
  Banana Bread in a Mug, 122
  Banana Granola Bites, 60
  Blueberry Pancake
    in a Mug, 40
  Brownie for One, 125
  Buffalo Chicken Flatbreads, 81
  Chewy Chocolate Chip
    Granola Bars, 36
  Chocolate Peanut Butter
    Mug Cake, 121
  Cobb Salad Pitas, 77
  Creamy Fettuccine Alfredo, 105
  Crispy Rice Bars, 128
  Everything Bagel Potato
    Chips, 48–49
  5-Minute Apple Crisp, 123
  French Toast in a Mug, 41
  Lemony Cod, 98
  Loaded Baked Potatoes, 90
  Microwave Apple Cinnamon
    Oatmeal, 38

Microwave Bacon, 44
Microwave BBQ Chicken
    Nachos, 114
Microwave Chicken
    Enchiladas, 92
Microwave Chocolate
    Chip Cookie, 120
Microwave Granola, 59
Microwave Kettle Corn, 57
Microwave Mac & Cheese, 91
Microwave Meat Loaf, 115
Microwave Parmesan
    Chicken, 93
Microwave Risotto, 89
Microwave Scrambled Eggs, 43
Microwave Spaghetti
    Marinara, 104
Mini Pepperoni Pizzas, 63
Sausage and Egg Breakfast
    Taquitos, 45
Sesame Ramen Salad, 70
S'mores Caramel Popcorn, 58
Southwest Black Bean
    Soup, 99
Vegetarian Burrito Bowls, 86
Vegetarian Chili, 87
Veggie Gyros, 73
Veggie Ramen, 88
Warm Apple Pie Dip, 52
Zesty Spaghetti Squash
    Salad, 102–103
Mincing, 9, 23
Mini-fridges, 8
Miso-Glazed Salmon, 116
Mixing, 20–21
Mocha Smoothie, 37

N

Nachos, Microwave BBQ
    Chicken, 114
No cook
    Apple Cranberry Yogurt
        Salad, 68
    Bacon and Blue Cheese
        Wedge Salad, 67

Banana Pudding Parfait, 126
Brussels Sprouts
    Cranberry Salad, 69
Chicken Caesar Wraps, 76
Chocolate Caramel
    Sundae, 127
Classic Guacamole, 55
Cookie Dough Dip, 53
Creamy Hummus, 56
Lemon Pepper Tuna
    Lettuce Wraps, 74
Mocha Smoothie, 37
No-Bake Cheesecake, 124
Nutty Broccoli Salad, 71
Pineapple Salsa, 54
Spicy Wasabi Trail Mix, 62
Strawberry Almond
    Overnight Oats, 39
Strawberry Pecan
    Quinoa Salad, 66
Tuna Salad Avocado Bowls, 72
Turkey Club Wraps, 75
Two-Ingredient Veggie Dip, 51
Ultimate Roast Beef
    Sandwiches, 80
Nutty Broccoli Salad, 71

O

Oats
    Chewy Chocolate Chip
        Granola Bars, 36
    Microwave Apple Cinnamon
        Oatmeal, 38
    Microwave Granola, 59
    Strawberry Almond
        Overnight Oats, 39
Ovens, 30. See also
    Toaster ovens
    Baked Chicken Tenders, 94
    Baked Ham and Cheese
        Sliders, 110–111
    Brown Sugar Garlic Pork
        Medallions, 112–113
    Cinnamon Roll-Ups, 129
    Cinnamon Tortilla Crisps, 50

Crispy Oven "Fried"
    Chicken, 108–109
Miso-Glazed Salmon, 116
Ravioli Lasagna, 106–107
Sausage and Egg Breakfast
    Taquitos, 45
Shawarma Roasted
    Chickpeas, 61
Spinach Pesto Flatbread
    Pizzas, 84

P

Pancake in a Mug, Blueberry, 40
Pans, 28–29
Pantry staples, 10–11
Parmesan Chicken,
    Microwave, 93
Pasta and noodles
    Creamy Fettuccine
        Alfredo, 105
    microwave cooking, 25
    Microwave Mac &
        Cheese, 91
    Microwave Spaghetti
        Marinara, 104
    Ravioli Lasagna, 106–107
    Sesame Ramen Salad, 70
    Veggie Ramen, 88
Peanut Butter Mug Cake,
    Chocolate, 121
Pecan Quinoa Salad,
    Strawberry, 66
Pepperoni Pizzas, Mini, 63
Pesto Flatbread Pizzas,
    Spinach, 84
Pineapple Salsa, 54
Pizza
    Buffalo Chicken
        Flatbreads, 81
    Mini Pepperoni Pizzas, 63
    Spinach Pesto Flatbread
        Pizzas, 84
Popcorn
    Microwave Kettle Corn, 57
    S'mores Caramel Popcorn, 58

Pork
  Brown Sugar Garlic Pork
    Medallions, 112–113
  Italian Pork Chops, 96–97
Potatoes
  Everything Bagel Potato
    Chips, 48–49
  Loaded Baked Potatoes, 90
Pots, 29
Preheating, 8
Pudding Parfait, Banana, 126

Q

Quesadillas, Bean and
  Cheese, 85
Quinoa Salad, Strawberry
  Pecan, 66

R

Recipes
  about, 31–32
  cooking without, 30–31
  reading, 18–19
Refrigerator staples, 11–12
Resting, 9
Rice
  microwave cooking, 25
  Microwave Risotto, 89
Rice Bars, Crispy, 128

S

Safety, 23
Salads
  Apple Cranberry Yogurt
    Salad, 68
  Bacon and Blue Cheese
    Wedge Salad, 67
  Brussels Sprouts
    Cranberry Salad, 69
  Cobb Salad Pitas, 77
  Nutty Broccoli Salad, 71
  Sesame Ramen Salad, 70
  Strawberry Pecan
    Quinoa Salad, 66
  Tuna Salad Avocado Bowls, 72

Zesty Spaghetti Squash
    Salad, 102–103
Salmon, Miso-Glazed, 116
Salsa, Pineapple, 54
Sandwiches and wraps
  Baked Ham and Cheese
    Sliders, 110–111
  Bean and Cheese
    Quesadillas, 85
  BLT Avocado Toast, 42
  Caprese Chicken Grilled
    Cheese Sandwiches, 78–79
  Chicken Caesar Wraps, 76
  Cobb Salad Pitas, 77
  Lemon Pepper Tuna
    Lettuce Wraps, 74
  Turkey Club Wraps, 75
  Ultimate Roast Beef
    Sandwiches, 80
  Veggie Gyros, 73
Sausage and Egg Breakfast
    Taquitos, 45
Sautéing, 9, 28
Searing, 9, 28
Seasoning, 9, 24
"Sell by" dates, 13
Sesame Ramen Salad, 70
Shawarma Roasted
    Chickpeas, 61
Shopping, 5
Simmering, 9, 29
Slicing, 9, 22
Smoothie, Mocha, 37
S'mores Caramel
    Popcorn, 58
Soups, stews, and chilis
  Southwest Black Bean
    Soup, 99
  Vegetarian Chili, 87
  Veggie Ramen, 88
Spaghetti Squash Salad,
    Zesty, 102–103
Spinach Pesto Flatbread
    Pizzas, 84
Standing, 9

Steaming, 29
Stirring, 20
Stoves
  Bean and Cheese
    Quesadillas, 85
  Brown Sugar Garlic Pork
    Medallions, 112–113
  Caprese Chicken Grilled
    Cheese Sandwiches, 78–79
  Italian Pork Chops, 96–97
  The Perfect Burger, 95
  Ravioli Lasagna, 106–107
Strawberries
  Strawberry Almond
    Overnight Oats, 39
  Strawberry Pecan
    Quinoa Salad, 66
Sundae, Chocolate
    Caramel, 127

T

Taquitos, Sausage and
    Egg Breakfast, 45
Toaster ovens, 8, 27–28.
    See also Ovens
  BLT Avocado Toast, 42
  Mini Pepperoni Pizzas, 63
Tomatoes
  BLT Avocado Toast, 42
  Caprese Chicken Grilled
    Cheese Sandwiches, 78–79
Tools, 6–7
Tortilla Crisps, Cinnamon, 50
Tossing, 21
Trail Mix, Spicy Wasabi, 62
Transferring, 9
Tuna
  Lemon Pepper Tuna
    Lettuce Wraps, 74
  Tuna Salad Avocado
    Bowls, 72
Turkey Club Wraps, 75

U

"Use by" dates, 13

V

Vegan
  Cinnamon Tortilla Crisps, 50
  Classic Guacamole, 55
  Creamy Hummus, 56
  Everything Bagel Potato
    Chips, 48–49
  Microwave Granola, 59
  Pineapple Salsa, 54
  Shawarma Roasted
    Chickpeas, 61
  Spicy Wasabi Trail Mix, 62
  Strawberry Almond
    Overnight Oats, 39
  Warm Apple Pie Dip, 52
Vegetables. *See also specific*
  microwave cooking, 25
  Two-Ingredient Veggie Dip, 51
  Veggie Gyros, 73
  Veggie Ramen, 88
Vegetarian. *See also* Vegan
  Apple Cranberry Yogurt
    Salad, 68
  Banana Bread in a Mug, 122
  Banana Granola Bites, 60
  Banana Pudding Parfait, 126
  Bean and Cheese
    Quesadillas, 85
  Blueberry Pancake
    in a Mug, 40
  Brownie for One, 125
  Brussels Sprouts
    Cranberry Salad, 69
  Chewy Chocolate Chip
    Granola Bars, 36
  Chocolate Caramel Sundae, 127
  Chocolate Peanut Butter
    Mug Cake, 121
  Cinnamon Roll-Ups, 129
  Cookie Dough Dip, 53
  Creamy Fettuccine Alfredo, 105
  5-Minute Apple Crisp, 123
  French Toast in a Mug, 41
  Microwave Apple Cinnamon
    Oatmeal, 38
  Microwave Chocolate
    Chip Cookie, 120
  Microwave Kettle Corn, 57
  Microwave Mac & Cheese, 91
  Microwave Risotto, 89
  Microwave Scrambled Eggs, 43
  Microwave Spaghetti
    Marinara, 104
  Mocha Smoothie, 37
  No-Bake Cheesecake, 124
  Nutty Broccoli Salad, 71
  Sesame Ramen Salad, 70
  Southwest Black Bean
    Soup, 99
  Spinach Pesto Flatbread
    Pizzas, 84
  Strawberry Pecan
    Quinoa Salad, 66
  Two-Ingredient Veggie Dip, 51
  Vegetarian Burrito Bowls, 86
  Vegetarian Chili, 87
  Veggie Gyros, 73
  Veggie Ramen, 88
  Zesty Spaghetti Squash
    Salad, 102–103

W

Wasabi Trail Mix, Spicy, 62
Whisking, 9, 21
Worth the wait
  Classic Guacamole, 55
  Miso-Glazed Salmon, 116
  Ravioli Lasagna, 106–107
  Shawarma Roasted
    Chickpeas, 61
  Strawberry Almond
    Overnight Oats, 39
Wraps. *See* Sandwiches
  and wraps

Y

Yogurt Salad, Apple
  Cranberry, 68

Acknowledgments

To my college roommates and friends, Elaine, Melanie, Emily, Gina, Stacy, and Jessica. I cherish the lifelong memories we've made.

To my parents, for getting me my first "kitchen" when I was two. I'll bet you had no idea it would all turn into this.

To Dina and Dan, my first sous chefs. How many mud pies, grass salads, and crazy food concoctions did we make while growing up?

To Annie Choi and the Callisto team, thank you for bringing this book to life. I'm so grateful for your guidance.

And, of course, to Jim and Joe, for being my support system and faithful cheerleaders. I love you guys!

About the Author

 **Christina Hitchcock** is the creator and owner of the popular food blog *It Is a Keeper* (ItIsAKeeper.com). Her passion is sharing quick and easy recipes for busy families using easy-to-find, everyday ingredients. Christina discovered her love for cooking by spending time with her grandmothers in the kitchen. Her award-winning recipes have been featured on television, in national magazines, and on numerous online sites. Christina lives in northeast Pennsylvania with her husband and son. Follow her on Facebook (@ItsAKeeper), Instagram, YouTube, Twitter, and Pinterest (@ItsAKeeperBlog).